Duel with the North Downs

GARETH PRICE

Copyright © 2020 Gareth Price

All rights reserved.

ISBN: 9798550518007

This book is dedicated to
Lesley Lewis and Dan Park
who volunteered at Knockholt Village Hall
on Saturday 8th August 2020.

CONTENTS

1	DNF	1
2	Gnarking Around	4
3	The time-honoured route	9
4	Unbroken	16
5	An oven-baked plan	23
6	Uncertainty	31
7	Knockholt	35
8	Only Love	39
9	Spencerville	42
10	Broken	47
11	The Medway Gap	51
12	'An entry fee'	57
13	The Old Road	62
14	Coldrum	67
	Accounts from other runners	*74*
	Thank you	*87*
	References	*89*

'There are primal things that move us…
of these… the least obvious but the most important is
The Road'

Hilaire Belloc - 'The Old Road'

1 DNF

It's high summer. Quarter past five in the afternoon. Still too hot for the birds to sing…

I'm making painstaking progress along the edge of a field, somewhere south-west of Knockholt Pound, in the far left-hand corner of Kent.

Midway through mile 48, my skin is coated in a sticky film of sweat that's been accumulating since I set off from Farnham at six o'clock this morning. The perspiration's picked up a layer of grime and dust from the Downs, making my legs a dirty brown colour. My tee-shirt's soaked through with sweat. If I'd dunked it in the pond we passed a while back, it wouldn't have been any wetter.

Earlier, I might have compared myself to Roosevelt's 'man in the arena… covered in dust and sweat and tears' (1) - but I'm not in the mood anymore. The number pinned to my shorts might say North Downs Way 100, but I'm struggling to make it to 50 miles. At this rate, the half-way village hall is still half an hour ahead. When I get there, I plan to hand in my number and drop from the race.

A stream of other competitors come by, one after the other, making me feel like a car that's broken down, coasting to a stop along the hard shoulder. In the spirit of solidarity, some of them throw a cheery 'alright buddy?' over their shoulder as they pass. No, I'm not alright. I'm done.

The heat has been too much, above 30 degrees for hours. On the exposed sections of chalky downs, with the sun reflecting back off the white rock, it's felt like being baked alive. At one point, just after Merstham, more like being microwaved. Pushing it for hour after hour in these temperatures has drained my energy and willpower away.

The hills have been too much too. The bigger ones - Box Hill, Colley and Botley – brutal but ok. Here the path has made it painfully obvious you'll be starting at the bottom of the escarpment, ignoring the steepness of the contours and making a sadistic beeline to the top. A steady walk has been acceptable, essential even. Along with enthusiastic cursing at the relentless climbing, the build-up of lactic acid in the legs, the top that never seems to come.

But it's the unnamed shorter hills that have properly got under my defences. The spiteful little blighter just after we crossed the A22, that guy being carted off in an ambulance shortly after. The unexpected, straight-up, hands-on-thighs job that stopped me in my tracks a mile or so back. These have been the killer.

I've also broken my number one rule. To recce the route (2). Go and suss out where the hills are, what the surface is like to run on and how it feels to be out in the landscape. Then the race is easier to visualise. Then you're better prepared for what's up ahead.

If I'd managed to recce these first 50 miles, I'd have been ready for the repeated ups and downs. In the know about how to pace the faster section between Colley Hill and Merstham. Aware of the 'Marathon des Sables' field that microwaved me on mile 36.

And I haven't eaten nearly enough. Centurion have played their part to perfection, putting on a race safely during the pandemic. But eliminating the risk of cross contamination has meant a reduced range of foods at the aid stations, and I haven't done enough to organise alternatives I know I'll be able to eat under duress. And I've felt too nauseous in the heat to keep solid food down. I've stayed on top of the salt tablets, the electrolyte sachets in my water, and had the odd bite from a Soreen bar, but otherwise it's been nil by mouth. And now a major calorie deficit has found me out.

I phone my brother, my most empathetic supporter, to break the news I'm completely wiped, I'm going to DNF.

In ultra circles everyone is respectful around these letters (3), careful not to spell them out. But that voice in my head - which I've spent three years learning to silence on these sorts of runs, and which is back with a vengeance – is very happy to do it for me in a mocking tone.

'DID NOT FINISH. Did-not-finish. Did not finish.'

Alright enough.

'How the mighty have fallen! Not much of an ultrarunner now are you? Have any of these people coming by read your book I wonder? Look the other way and they won't see your face'

Eventually I'm on the main road heading downhill into the village. A final half-hearted jogging effort quickly peters out. I cast my mind back to the videos previous entrants have made about the race on YouTube (4). There's normally an assortment of well-wishers gathered round the hall at Knockholt, giving each runner a round of applause.

'You won't want that. You don't deserve it mate. Hand in your number without being noticed and then slink off home on the train with your tail between your legs.'

I climb the steps to the hall and tell the volunteer in the face mask I want to DNF. My finger hovers over the button on my watch, ready to stop it and bring this suffering to an end.

2 GNARKING AROUND

Nine months earlier. I'm in a muddy field with a trig point in it on the crest of the Chiltern Hills, down jacket on, breath condensing in the November air. There's a frosty sunrise, mist lingering across the nearby valleys, ice crystals on the gloopy leaf mulch underfoot.

The ultra community has come out en masse to volunteer, support and run in the last Centurion event of 2019 – the Wendover Woods 50 miler. All around me people are greeting old friends – shaking hands, hugging each other, generally carefree. There's a big marquee and the steady thrum of a generator. I chat to Brian and Spencer, fellow Thames Path centurions, milling around to keep warm in the queue for a coffee from the pop-up café.

The race is five 10-mile laps of the woods. Two thousand feet of climbing per lap. A few weekends before - in typically generous fashion - Brian had led me and a few other rookies for a recce, stepping in for Spencer after he had car trouble.

Wendover is famous for its Gruffalo, its affectionately named awkward bits – 'Gnarking Around', 'Root Canal', 'The Boulevard of Broken Dreams' (5). Brian gives us a VIP tour. We meet some of the female ultra running elite on our way round. Anna who came second overall in the 100 mile race a few months before is showing Sophie the ropes. Sophie goes on to win the women's race (6).

Maybe because it's only one lap, I come away thinking how much fun it was. I give some of the remaining sections my own names – 'Lost Dog Descent' – Con's Sprocker Spaniel had found something way more interesting than our run and vanished for a while; 'Sandwich Hill' the place to chow down supplies picked up at the end of each lap; and 'Where's Brian?' – the up and down job our host sensibly avoided by walking round the bottom.

Training has gone to plan, and I'm stood amidst a crowd of several hundred runners at the start line feeling chipper.

A klaxon sounds and we're off. The narrow road funnels the field into a tightly packed group and with a mile on easy terrain first-up, we accelerate away, along through the trees, around the café, down by the Gruffalo, shooting by Stu March, the official photographer snapping away, the flashes triggering a surge of adrenaline, a sudden spurt as we all feel part of the spectacle. Then there's a sudden deceleration. The route veers abruptly left. We concertina back into a queue to ascend a muddy bank. Seconds lost, but something liberating about having a reason to stop and walk so early in a race.

Onto smaller single-track trails, watching for roots and the thicker patches of mud that need four-wheel drive mode. Weave through the intersecting log piles, then speed up daringly down the ramp and narrow gully of Lost Dog Descent. Put the brakes on at the bottom and turn left up the Ridgeway climb. A minute or two later make a right and pick it up down Powerline Descent. Careful though, it steepens alarmingly in the middle and there are steps and a gate to negotiate before letting your legs carry you across the field in a giant arc left towards where we saw the rainbow.

Soon we're girding our loins for the vicious ramp up into a natural amphitheatre in the woods, groaning at the gradient of over 25%, teetering left and slip sliding our way up and around a tree. And after some downtime, repeating the effort a few minutes later up the similarly steep Go Ape Climb, with a gaggle of well-wishers gathered at the top.

Next up, the beautifully runnable downhill section along a windy single track through conifers, the slow down to pick our way across the ankle-breaking Root Canal, then the sprint along to the timing mat at Hale Lane aid station just before the hour mark.

Half-way round. No need to stop this early on. Push on up the hill beyond. The field's spreading out now. Crest the top and enjoy the mile or so of clean running down and round the Boulevard of Broken Dreams - with its promise of very painful quads on later laps.

Oh my God 'The Snake' is unrelenting. So, take a breather on the gentle jog round Hill Fort Loop, but put your foot down again on the other long descent, getting ready to come to a halt for the sharp right up Gnarking Around – the steepest climb on the course.

Step over the fallen log then try and pick your way up whichever side has the least mud, accept it's going to stick to your shoes, and marvel at the 44% gradient while trying to keep the panting under control. Pull a face for Brian offering encouragement at the top and enjoy 'The Reward' a lovely trundle back down to get the legs going again.

Finally, stomp your way up 'Railing in the Years,' climb over the stile and jog your way across Trig Point Field and the ten-mile timing mat.

Back in the marquee with the first lap done in just under two hours. Hand your water bottles to a friendly volunteer to refill, and head off again for more of the same.

Lap Two. Increasingly absorbed in this varied, rarely flat, trail-running funfair ride. Gaining temporary traction from earth, bedrock, grass then mud. Feeling the freedom of arms-flailing brakes-off downhill running. Experiencing a heart-pounding blood rush pressing as hard as possible up hill after hill which seems even steeper than first time round.

Back in the marquee with the second lap done in a smidge under four hours.

Midway through lap three, calves cramping up, tiredness creeping in. Marathon distance. Time to make use of Hale Lane, grab some handfuls of salty food. Be sure to eat those ham sandwiches and crisps on the uphill after.

Breathe it all in, inhale something comforting and familiar in this mulchy smell of Autumn on the afternoon air...

Through the marquee again. Stu McLaughlin finding me my drop bag in double quick time, giving me an update on Spencer, telling me I'm 'doing well.'

Lap four in fast fading light. Taking care on my way down Lost Dog Descent in the gloaming.

Thinking back to the challenges of the last few months - me and Ilaria separating, getting used to being home alone for the first time in 13 years, but grateful to remain custodian of Lily the cat.

Slow jogging down Powerline Descent. Headtorch on for the climb up into the amphitheatre.

Remembering how pissed Lily had been at the upheaval when we'd adopted her the year before. Positioning herself on the stairs for the first few days hissing at anyone who tried to go past. But settling in on the condition she was allowed to be in charge. Going on to become Queen of our road, frequently admired by passers-by.

Plodding up Go Ape Climb then coaxing myself into a jog down the trail through the trees. Watching my footing along Root Canal.

With just the two of us, she'd taken to sleeping alongside me in the bed. A self-contained ginger and white unit, grudgingly allowing me to fiddle with her ear, letting me marvel at how soft it was. And she'd wait for me halfway down the road as I walked back from the station, escorting me back to the house with a where-have-you-been expression on her face.

Running through Hale Lane again. Marching up the hill the other side. Jogging down the Boulevard of Broken Dreams.

Then the message the week before the race to say she'd been run over. The news of internal injuries. The decision to put her down. Burying her little ball of fur in the woods.

Grinding round the rest of lap four, powered by the rawness of the grief...

It's later now and I'm on lap five in the dark, my frosted breath drifting around in the beam of my headtorch.

The other competitors are spread out around the course, leaving me alone with the owls. Despite everything I feel a semblance of peace. Running gives me an outlet, a way of coming to terms with what's been lost.

Although the temperature has dropped, I'm moving fast enough to avoid putting on a fleece, likely to beat my target time.

Here's Kerry, friendly and encouraging at Hale Lane, a South Downs centurion herself. She offers me one of the cheesecakes, the stash she's brought with her to supplement the aid station supplies. She's saving one for Spencer as he comes through.

Onto the last five miles - one more Snake, a final bit of Gnarking Around, and then stride up Railing in the Years for the last time, sprint in across the field and stop the clock on 11 hours and 13 minutes.

Ian Hammett – the guy who won the Thames Path 100 earlier in the year – hands me my medal. Then he notices my headtorch is still on inside the brightly lit marquee. He reaches across and turns it off.

3 THE TIME-HONOURED ROUTE

I'm by the dual carriageway in Farnham, and a Centurion volunteer is reaching towards me again. This time wearing full PPE and waving a temperature gun. My heartbeat shoots up for a second or two while he checks the reading… then he gives me the thumbs up sign.

I've got the all clear, had my photo taken at the North Downs Way trailhead and picked up my tracker. There's no reason to procrastinate… Apart from feeling the effects of a fitful night's sleep, the rude interruption of the four-thirty alarm, just as I finally dozed off. And needing to get used to the weight of the pack on my back – full to the brim with mandatory kit, extra food and water, bits and pieces to protect me from the heat.

I dawdle for another 30 seconds or so, then remembering the very clear instructions not to hang around, walk down to the start, press go on my watch and begin jogging towards Ashford.

It is exhilarating to be back in the race arena, to have a 100 mile race number pinned to my shorts, to imagine my siblings in Hong Kong, Friern Barnet and Burnham-on-Sea, assorted friends and colleagues, watching my red dot pulse into action on their screens. I'll be following in the footsteps of traders, drovers, monarchs and pilgrims (7). Turns out I'll be following in the footsteps of Mr. Giacomo Squintani too, as he comes past me almost immediately, with the bit between his teeth. And of course, he's wearing his lucky lime green compression socks.

For a moment, my racehorse instinct kicks in and I'm tempted to tuck in on his shoulder. We are fellow Thames Path centurions after all. But I know he's fitter and faster than me and there are over 103 miles to go. There's no need to fall for such a schoolboy error this early on. I settle back to my 10-minute mile pace.

Race Director James Elson put in an appearance at the rolling start, presiding over this triumph of attention to detail. He's sent us four emails, posted a 24-minute briefing on YouTube (8), appeased worried landowners by shifting the action away from busier bits of trail. Up ahead 95 volunteers wearing masks and nitrile gloves are safely setting up 12 Covid-secure aid stations. At some point in the next few days, maybe he and his team will get to feel proud, realise the courage, humanity and logistical brilliance they've shown in making this race happen.

We switch from trail to road. My watch vibrates to say the first mile is done. There's a hefty little hill up ahead – Giacomo, disappears away in the distance, running it. I'll be walking these thank you very much!

A few days earlier, trying to get my head around the forecast 34 degrees, I had a Zoom call with my sister in Hong Kong. She helped me break the race into four chunks and between here and Box Hill, according to the notes in my pocket, I'm going to stay 'Relaxed.' So, I focus on letting the rhythm of the running settle me down, and, for the first time in days, my mind starts to quieten.

We travel through a field of crops, picking our way along its gently rising left hand edge, then jog in and out of woods, negotiating some easy ups and downs. I'm letting the trail unfold in front of me, ticking off ten, eleven-

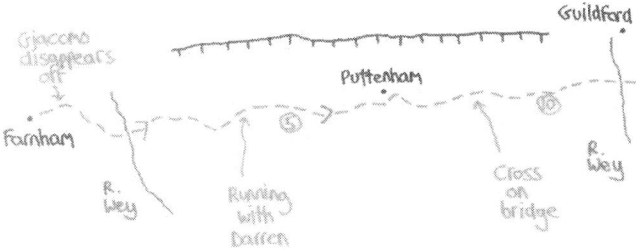

minute miles without worrying about the time. There's suddenly the unmistakeable smell of tea – as if someone's brewing up in one of the fields alongside. But there's no-one else around - it must be emanating from the earth, still a little damp from an overnight shower.

Runners are streaming east through the quiet of the early morning, watching for the Centurion signs, the garlands of marker tape, which show the way. The collective effort helps - it feels at times, like I'm being tugged along by an unseen current. And although I'm often alone, there are interludes alongside others.

Darren is self-contained, friendly - a volunteer from previous years, marking the last section of the course - happy to compare notes on the harder parts up ahead. A mile or two further on, just before Puttenham, Sam is ebullient, all infectious enthusiasm, telling me about the time he ran the Sparthalon. And then there's Rob. Rob with an aura about him, the feel of a 21st century folk hero - one who bagged a world record in this race a few years before. I say how much I liked his video (9), that it made me cry. He's pleased.

People have passed this way for centuries. Hilaire

Belloc traced the ancient byway along the North Downs, the probable prehistoric track between Stonehenge and the Channel ports, tracking the line of chalky hills, avoiding the supposedly impenetrable wood on the Weald. He called it 'The Old Road' and came along here on his research, convinced this was the time-honoured route (10). There's a nearby Neolithic tumulus on Puttenham Heath, giving his argument ammunition.

In the Middle Ages pilgrims may well have passed along here too, travelling to Thomas Becket's shrine at Canterbury (11). And on that note, it's hard to miss the giant cross on the front of the bridge as we run underneath the A3. Maybe a blessing for us runners would be in order!

In the humid air my skin feels clammy, but at least there's a bit of wind around. Time to take one of my little salt tablets, top up on electrolytes, remember neglecting them on a felt-like-I'd-hit-a-brick-wall long run a few weeks before.

We descend into Guildford for a scenic, all-too-quickly-over, stretch along the River Wey – the first of the river valleys cutting through the Downs. There's a bridge across to Shalford Park, then the crews are lined up on both sides, giving us a little sprinkling of applause - which I could lap up all day.

Our route ramps steeply up through Chantry Wood, the first major climb and a chance to test the legs. Now the sunken path has a proper here-through-the-ages feel. And at the top of the hill there's been a stopover place of worship for at least 800 years (12).

There are 360-degree views to take in when we get there. They make it tempting to stay awhile. Occupying the space and set in its own walled grounds, St Martha's Church is like something out of a film set. The sort of place where the hero arrives on horseback – not by jogging!

I'm thinking about the aid station and press on, calling across to alert a bloke heading in the wrong direction.

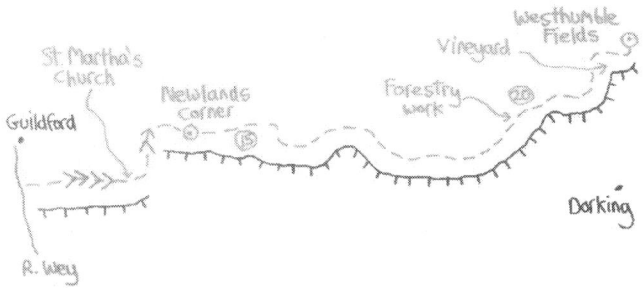

There's thick sand around as we head steeply downhill again and my knee feels very uncomfortable suddenly. Put it out of your mind, that sort of pain often wears off.

There's open country at the top of the next hill, the trail tracking just below the crest of Albury Downs. We've been gaining height since Guildford and now nearly 600 feet up, 14 miles out from Farnham, the Downs take on their distinctive shape, lording it over sweeping views to the south. It's a quintessential English scene – rolling hills, rural farmhouses and late summer woods - crying out for an orchestral soundtrack, something by Vaughan Williams perhaps…

Stu, the race photographer, is there in the distance with a long zoom lens. The steep camber of the slope means I keep watching my footing, but I manage to pull a sheepish smile for the camera.

On to Newlands Corner – with its distinct day out from London vibe. These Centurion 100s tend to have an Agatha Christie moment at some point and this is reportedly the spot she parked her car late in 1926 and disappeared for ten days (13). Mysterious!

I pull to a halt at the back of a queue of runners, carefully positioned two metres apart, everyone's first experience of a socially distanced aid station. One guy gestures dismissively and runs off – I'm not sure what he's going to do for water – but clearly he has a plan?!

A volunteer calls me forward to squirt myself with hand gel. Then I'm filling my bottles, fiddling cack-handedly with the tap on the water container as tiredness creeps in. Not even nine o'clock, yet it feels like I've been up for hours. I have been up for hours!

Anna is helping here as well, a welcome friendly face - even if she is a couple of metres away. She recognises me from the Wendover recce - 'well done Gareth, looking good - nice to be out racing again?!' 'For sure!' She counsels me about taking it easy in the hot hours ahead.

Her pep talk gives me an unexpected boost and the first stretch out from the aid station is sublime, running along wide-open trails through the woods on the top of the Downs. Up here, the air is a fraction cooler, and I can feel the breeze on my face. A mountain biker comes by super-fast, allowing us just enough time to sidestep smartly out of the way.

Then we switch onto a single-track trail which winds through coppiced woods. Debris from forestry work spills repeatedly onto the undulating path, slowing things down, creating complications, a need to concentrate harder on where you put your feet.

Afterwards, chugging across Ranmore Common, the views open out again and we can see down to Dorking. The crews are here once more, dotted amongst the daytrippers, and I'm beginning to think I've missed a trick by not organising this support for myself...

Jog down a rather grand driveway, then along past a vineyard. Hard not to associate these with the bottom part of France, the Mediterranean. The south facing slopes must be a suntrap... Forget about that, focus on this blissfully smooth downhill stretch, switch off from the more technical trail, and let your legs carry you to a sweet spot just on the cusp of out of control...

Ten minutes or so later I reach the bottom and pull up at the back of the queue for Westhumble aid station. Just under 24 miles done - nicely inside my 4 hour 30 minute schedule.

While I wait for one of the do-it-yourself tables to free up, there's time to check the messages on my phone and WhatsApp my brother to tell him he's right about me trying to get some faster miles in before the heat makes it impossible.

There's a chance to take stock, think about the next stage of my plan. But I'm suddenly really hot, the closeness of the traffic on the A24 feels grating, and the two metre gap between me and the guy in front is bringing all the upheavals of the last six months back to the surface again.

4 UNBROKEN

I've got 2020 all figured out. I'll recover from Wendover, build on what I've learnt, and throw everything at the South Downs Way 100 in early June. It's the most scenic, popular Centurion race, taking in some of the best trail running in the country.

Training is going well through the first few months. I'm up to 60-mile weeks again, building a handful of regular running partners too.

When he's back from Germany, taking a break from holiday home renovation, me and my friend Michael are evenly matched for pace, and always have energising runs in each other's company.

My brother's interest in the sport is growing. We go out for a few miles together on my visits to Somerset and I can see his enthusiasm first-hand, the obvious impact running has on his wellbeing.

And then there's Wednesday night club, eight milers along the abandoned railway line in Forest Row with my friend Liz from work.

At the beginning of March, Liz and I do the Lydd 20-mile race together. She's training for the Brighton Marathon and this is a chance for her to do a longer run on a flat out-and-back route, sort her race routine.

But bad luck means this is the day her period starts, and she has a tough time of it during the second ten miles. She pulls out a gutsy performance anyway – occasional breaks to take a gel, then digging deep to carry on when she's not feeling like it. She comes home in the top third of the field in a respectable time of just over three hours. It's a privilege to be alongside her and witness how she finds a way through.

And of course, as I'm sure most people do, we take the whole race day thing for granted. Travelling there in the car together, milling around with hundreds of others before the mass start, grabbing cups of water and jelly babies from volunteers along the verge...

A fortnight later, with the graphs climbing exponentially, our normal day-to-day lives are upended as we retreat en masse into lockdown.

I have a fairly secure, meaningful job fundraising for London Youth. It can be done from home. I have access to the countryside for the allotted exercise slot, decent living space in my terraced house, and my friends and family get through the first peak largely unscathed.

But I find it hard to handle being by myself nearly 24 hours a day. Lockdown adds a new layer of intensity to being home alone. I crave human contact, especially during those first few months of confinement, when the rules are strictest.

Before Covid, there was this daily dose of unthinking physical interaction, a taken for granted exchange of human touch – the occasional mutually beneficial hug, consoling hand on the shoulder, or kiss on the cheek. Now, without any warning, it's all completely gone. Replaced by unease, lost bearings and a corrosive emptiness which comes and goes like a tide.

I had no idea how much I would miss looking at another person's face when we're in the same room. Once this experience is unequivocally taken away, remembering it reminds me of the comfort you get from gazing at a log fire.

At least we all seem to be more tuned into each other's mental health. And when I find myself sobbing for apparently no reason on an unreal April day, I realise just how much I need to be tuned into my own.

Running has always been one of my favourite ways of engaging with the world. Now it becomes essential self-preservation, an outlet where although I'm alone, I no longer feel lonely.

The once-a-day trip outside the house takes on a powerful dimension. And during those surreal first forty days, there's a long spell of settled weather, day after day of sunshine. Spring is sprung with an intensity none of us have experienced before...

One evening, I head out the door and set off up Bird-in-Eye Hill. I take some deep breaths, immerse myself in the exercise. The contrast between indoors and out is intense - a sensory overload - like coming round after an anaesthetic.

I run through a tunnel of luminous green, getting an eyeful of chlorophyll, of flickering translucent light. A tonic after eight hours screen time. Out in the open again, the sky is crystal clear, unbroken by vapour trails, shimmering like the surface of a swimming pool.

I roll over the crest of the hill, feel the breeze on my face for the first time, and savour the prospect of the hundred and fifty foot plummet down to the Tickerage Stream. The surface of the road drops beneath my feet, and I relax and speed up, going with the flow of whirligig legs.

All too soon the descent is done, and crossing the bridge in the bottom of the valley, I get a glimpse of dark meandering stream, framed through an arch of spoon-shaped leaves.

A mile and a half uphill. My momentum leaks away

and, with the breeze now nowhere to be seen, I'm more aware of the heat of the afternoon.

It's a relief to get to the top, swing round to the right. This new lane is narrow and overgrown, and I accelerate down again. There's a claret-coloured copper beech by a chocolate box house, red campion and forget-me-nots nestling in the grass, colour splattered everywhere – a living breathing Jackson Pollock painting.

I'm heading further out from civilisation, into one of those land-that-time-forgot corners of countryside that Sussex does so well.

Down in the bottom, I weave through a shadowy dell, and after a steep pull up the other side, stop on the spur of the moment.

The evening has a medieval feel to it. The birdsong comes in waves - mellifluous, then strident, then wobbly. In its absence the silence is deafening. The missing aircraft noise is palpable.

Up ahead the road disappears into the ether. There's a row of backlit beech that give this stretch a cathedral-like quality, and amplify the birdsong.

There's a strong sense of time standing still, increased fusion with nature (14). I want to stay where I am - lost in a bermuda triangle of land, enjoying the hiatus and soaking in the intensity of being alive…

There are other moments too, amidst this strictest period of lockdown, when, with no-one else around, there's the faint, but unmistakeable impression of nature being given some unbroken breathing space, even occasionally allowed to have the upper hand. It's as if we've all pressed pause on the Anthropocene. Others notice it as well.

It reminds me of an ecology field trip to Rum, twenty years before – an ancient volcano, an island in the Inner Hebrides that has no cars, that's virtually devoid of human habitation, a place where the air has a sweet and intense purity (15).

The night of my 30th birthday we sat near the top of a mountain at three in the morning, quietly taking in the experience of Manx Shearwaters returning to their burrows after a day of Atlantic fishing. They were listening out for the distinct, plaintiff cries of their partners, their homing device, and then crash-landing clumsily into the side of the hill all around us. In the beams of our torches, the little black and white birds got to their feet with a no-harm-done kind of bravado.

Elsewhere on the island other animals and birds seemed to have taken back control. Maybe they never gave it up in the first place. Out on a walk a Golden Eagle comes for an effortless fly-by, checking our party out, giving us an ice-cold mid-glide glare, signalling this is her domain.

I wrote poetry on the boat back to Mallaig – something about a song on the wind, only hearing it when you let the notes fly free. And then came the almost crushingly painful contrast of the concrete right angles of the Fort William shopping centre we stopped in on the drive home.

The South Downs Way 100 is cancelled. Centurion have held on as long as they can but by the end of April it's obviously no longer viable to run it.

There are no races for any of us. I, like tens of thousands of other runners, have been training for months - now supposedly for nothing. Maybe not. Towards the end of 'The Way of the Runner', Adharanand Finn's ekiden – his set-piece relay race - gets called off because of a snowstorm, but he's philosophical:

'There is no race. It's very Zen... Those days of running are not wasted if we don't run a race. If you miss your exam at the end of a course, it doesn't mean you haven't learnt anything' (16)

Many do learn. Centurion put on a life-enhancing 'One Community' virtual challenge at the end of May. Nearly 4,000 people from around the world record their times from 5k to 100 miles (17).

Many use the race-free summer to reach unprecedented, liberating, once-in-a-lifetime levels of fitness. Jon Kelly sets a fastest known time for the Pennine Way (18), then Damien Hall beats it (19). Sabrina Verjee does the best time for a woman. Then becomes the first woman to run the Wainwrights non-stop (20). And Dan Lawson pulls off a superhuman, deeply moving, deeply harrowing Land's End to John O'Groats record run, inside ten days (21).

I'm no match for these legends of the sport but I surf a wave of fitness too myself. Aged 51, I manage back to back sub-four marathons for the first time: 3.49 the first day, 3.47 the second. I never imagined being able to do this, recovering quickly enough. But I find myself flooded with euphoria midway through mile 22 second time round, sprinting like my life depends on it, like I was born to run.

I had tentatively signed up for the North Downs Way 100, pencilled in for the beginning of August, hoping restrictions would have lifted sufficiently by then to make racing doable again. Now the email comes through from Centurion to say it is going ahead - they've put social distancing protocols in place to make it safe.

I refocus on this race, start imagining how it might feel to finish on the athletics track in the stadium in Ashford. The last 15 miles or so - running south-east along the Pilgrims Way at the bottom of the Downs – is known terrain from growing up in Kent. I went back to walk the section from Lenham to Eastwell last summer. Me and my friend Ace had a companionable day out, enjoying our journey along a track that had clearly been there for centuries. It brought back memories from one of my first runs in the early 80s – a cross-country from Swadelands School up to, and around, the giant chalk cross on the hillside.

But the North Downs Way also has a reputation as the

hardest of the four regular 100 mile races – nearly 11,000 feet of ascent, low numbers of 'One Day' buckles normally dished out. My friend Peter Dennett walked long stretches of the earlier section and found the constant ups and downs 'a royal pain in the back side'. Others have told how soul-destroying it can be, if and when, the last section of the race degenerates into a death march (22).

In for a penny in for a pound. I've got enough miles in my legs, and there's still over four weeks left to recce the route...

5 AN OVEN-BAKED PLAN

It's about 11 o'clock when the sun starts to burn off the cloud and the heat of the day makes its presence properly felt for the first time. I'm on a long drag just east of Box Hill and stop and put on my sunglasses, slip on my new foreign-legion-style hat...

The last 10 days have been dominated by an unhealthy obsession with the increasingly dramatic-looking weather forecast. The predicted temperature keeps going up. It finally settles on 34 degrees for Merstham mid-afternoon.

There's a cluster of not-wanting-to-sound-too-alarming-but-are-you-still-doing-it messages from friends and family. #NDW100 entrants on social media are trying to downplay things, posting links to arm guards and specialist sun-cream and super thin socks.

All of this is accompanied by a fair degree of wide-awake at three in the morning, sensible when you think about it, stomach-churning fear. Is this viable? What are the symptoms for heatstroke? How is it different from heat exhaustion? Do I need to make a will?

A lot of advice is flying around. It's calming to compare notes online with Andy, Chris, Ally and the others, to counter fear with positive thinking, to make a list of ways to beat the heat.

Firstly, it is physiologically and physically possible. Many of the ultras in Europe and the USA take place in these sorts of temperatures. The Western States is almost invariably run in hotter conditions.

And I've run in the heat before. Those three weeks in Greece last summer, writing and running. The temperature in the 30s every day, cajoling myself to jog the 1,000 foot climb up to Drosopigi. Sweating buckets but enjoying the intensity of the challenge, the reward of cooler air on the hilltop and then the run back down. I knew I would eventually have to do a 100 in the heat and figured it would be good conditioning.

There's relief in remembering a key passage from Deena Kastor's book. Physiologists helping her and the American Olympic team prepare for the inevitably high temperatures during the Athens Marathon, emphasised being extremely fit as the best defence (23). After months of lockdown running, I know I'm in the best shape I've ever been. There's some comfort in that.

A key part of everyone's plan is to have patience on the section I'm on now, allowing enough time to be really slow on this second marathon, the long up and down miles between Box Hill and Knockholt in the hottest hours of the day.

And as the heatwave rolls in the day before, there's a helpful WhatsApp message from my 11-year-old niece Rachel. She's just burnt her arm on the back of the car and when I confirm I'm still doing the race she advises me 'get lots of water.' Good shout Rachey!

I'm back on it, engrossed in the terrain, thinking about Colley Hill, the next big landmark up ahead.

Despite my fixation with recceing the route, there's also something wonderful about heading into the

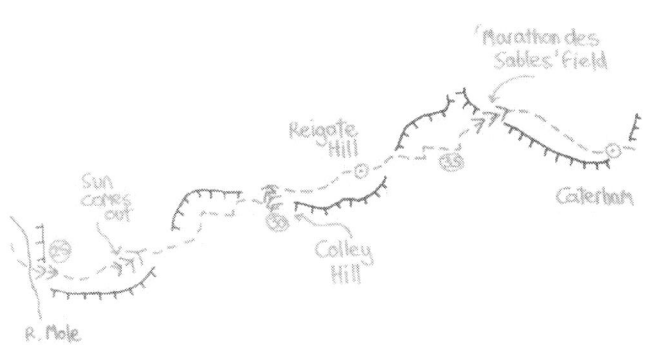

unknown, surrendering to the wriggle and rhythm of the path; forever unsure how long it will stay up here on the crest, what lies round the next corner, when sun will give way to shade; and coupled with that, not knowing the limits of my endurance in this weather.

A chalky downhill gully demands care but is also fun, it's enjoyable to take the brakes off again and feel like I'm on top of things. At the bottom we follow a pavement along a busy road but we're soon back on the trail again.

We turn north, the path enclosed between two fields. The main scarp slope of the Downs is dead ahead. Are we going up it? Not for now.

The Centurion signs send us right along a single-track trail through the woods at the bottom of the hill. It's narrow and overgrown in places, hard to get a rhythm going, I slow down to have a gel.

And then, near the end of mile 30, here's what I've been waiting for - the hard-left turn, the distinctive wire mesh fence on the right, sandy brush and yew needles on the floor. Unrelenting Colley Hill, ranked by local expert Ivor, as one of the hardest climbs on the course – 21% gradient, 280 feet of up.

The next six minutes are intense. There's a

straightforward, single-minded feel to the challenge – get to the top as fast as you can without going into the red. I'm sweating buckets and can hear the hum of traffic on the M25 by the time the gradient eases.

There's then a chance to draw breath - a sedate, parkland stretch along the top of Reigate Hill. Someone coming the other way tells us it's 1.1 miles to the next aid station. Is it necessary to be quite so damn accurate? A mile would have been more manageable! Next up, the ornate columns and shady interior of the Inglis Memorial. It's tempting to stop, but I jog gently past.

There's a much shorter queue at Reigate - mile 32. I sanitise, fill my bottles, search for something to eat. I haven't had the bag of crisps from Westhumble eight miles before – but don't want them anymore. It dawns on me how much I'm missing watermelon, cocktail sausages – my go to first few mouthfuls in pre-Covid races. I have a satsuma instead, but it immediately disagrees with me.

It's not all bad. One of the volunteers gives me a beautiful little bag of ice. I can't hug them, but I can have it sat at the top of my back for the next half an hour or so.

Off again, there's an eminently runnable downhill track, a chance to go a bit faster through miles 33 and 34. We wind our way through the grounds of a private school, across a cricket pitch, over the heaving-with-traffic M25, and through the churchyard at Merstham. Then comes the familiar entry into Rockshaw Road. I've driven a minibus full of kids along here enough times in my instructing days. There's a bloke in an adjoining garden, spraying runners with a hose, if they wish to partake. Yes please, I'll have some of THAT thank you very much!

I'm still in the zone, running past the long line of crews parked up along the pavement on the right hand side, and crossing underneath the M23. I congratulate myself on digging deep for three faster miles, and note with satisfaction, my staying power, my developing prowess as an ultrarunner, the endurance I've managed to develop...

And now the trap is sprung. The time is ten past one and the reported temperature is 34 degrees centigrade.

In front of me is an arid rocky field with the sun reflecting straight off the flinty bedrock, the North Downs Way rising for hundreds of feet across the middle of it. Marathon Des Sables eat your heart out. It's time to burn.

Over the next eight and a half minutes my awareness narrows to the few feet of dusty rubble in front of me, my heart rate goes through the roof, and various brain functions – like remembering important stuff – short-circuit and shut down completely.

When I do eventually get to the top – I'm panting hard, my legs are like jelly, and I'm not sure who I am anymore.

Walk slowly for a while. There's some relief coming - the route's heading into the shade. Allow yourself a slower up and down mile, then speed up to try and pass a family of walkers. Nope, there's not much momentum from that. Not the big shot now, are you?!

There's more merciful shade trundling down a road. My watch vibrates with a 13 minute mile. The numbers don't mean much anymore. Up again, this time to the aid station on Caterham Hill.

Just under 8 hours in, feeling dozy, queuing in the sun...

A volunteer stops me just in the nick of time as I'm about to squirt hand sanitiser into my drinking cup.

I stand at the table of food, and in an effort not to hold up the socially distanced queue of tired runners, shove more stuff into my backpack without realising I'm not actually eating any of it.

I force myself to have one of my rehydration drinks – the electrolyte sachets you get from the chemists. I requisition one of the camping chairs, take ten minutes to regroup. There's a man lying down in the shade, not moving very much. I recognise one of the volunteers, still smiling behind her mask, despite the heat. It's Lou, last spotted at Abingdon aid station, mile 91 on the Thames 100 (24). She says hi and how are you doing? Ok, I guess. Thank you.

No time like the present. Off again, dropping down through the woods to the bridge over the A22.

Now there's just up and down on repeat, like being in a washing machine, battered and sucked around without much control. My physiology is out of synch. Maybe it's just hunger knock. Momentum and other runners sometimes pull me along, but I'm finding it harder to ignore the obvious fact I'm slowing down dramatically.

Winders Hill - the sort of short spiteful climb the North Downs specialise in. Only 100 feet of up, but 20% in places. The straw that broke the camel's back? There's a runner in trouble to the side. Stopped and doubled over, not wanting help. He picks himself up and carries on but a mile or two later there's an ambulance by the roadside and I know it's him.

Forget about pace - pointless to worry about some arbitrary minute per mile goal along here. Not long ago you'd been going four and a half hours. Now it will soon be nine. Where's the afternoon gone? Hill after hill – coming at you like punches in a fight – all your energy draining away.

The Downs become more untamed hereabouts. I'm suddenly surrounded by towering chalk cliffs which seem to be fighting against civilisation, against me, asserting their wildness. Try to concentrate on the way ahead. Negotiate this almost vertical, vertigo-inducing descent down towards the railway line, heading up to East Croydon, disappearing into a tunnel hidden from sight underneath me. If I trip, I might tumble onto the tracks below. Grab the wooden handrail, and curse at steps that are, somehow, too far apart.

At the bottom there's more flint-covered fields, more baking hot masochism, an even more sedentary tempo.

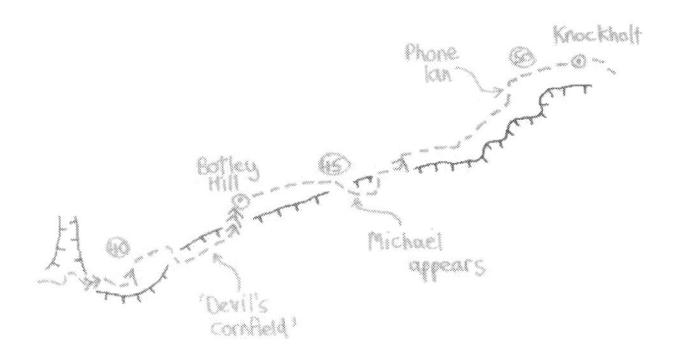

During the post-mortem, this stretch, and stretch is the right word, will hereby be known as the Devil's Cornfield.

Power walk up Botley Hill, the highest hill on the course, zig-zag if you need to, hands on thighs. Despite everything you're passing a few people.

At the top, there's a long queue for the aid station in the sun. The volunteers aren't getting any shade either. Graham has completed the race himself (25) and is here in the heat, giving back to the sport.

I fill my water bottles clumsily and stagger over to squat on the only vacant log. Force myself to think about electrolytes, fix another lukewarm rehydration drink, stir it ineffectively with my first two fingers, all the powder stubbornly circling at the bottom.

13 minutes go by. I nearly don't get up again. Laura sends me a text message to tell me I'm 'doing brilliantly.' That's not how I'd describe it, but it means a lot any way and it's nice to hear from her.

Eventually I find the will to move and force myself to a doddery upright position, legs nearly giving way. Sinead, wearing a high-viz jacket that seems rather cutely too big for her, gives me an arms-wide virtual hug as I cross the road on the way out.

The part of my brain that remembers stuff has shut up shop for the afternoon. All I can do is propel myself forward somehow. Rolling gingery down a hill I imagine my friend Michael stood on the left-hand side like a mirage. But the mirage is talking to me, it is actually him, come with Michelle to see if I'm ok. He offers me a top up of water from his van by the roadside, before sending me on my way.

Mile 47, the trail heads up another hill, rising almost vertically from the stile. Why can't we go along the ridge rather than up and down it all the time? I slow to a snail's pace, exchange a few sluggish words with a fellow sufferer alongside. She explains she's had enough, she'll be getting the train home from the 50-mile mark at Knockholt.

Train home? What a fantastic idea! I could do that too, make all of this go away. In a couple of hours, I could be sat in the bath relaxing all these worn out muscles, then sleeping in my own bed....

I tell myself snap out of it, you've bonked, you need food. I sit down and look at the banana Soreen bar at the top of my pack. The first bite makes me nauseous. I can't eat any of it.

It takes me 24 minutes to do mile 48. My mind is shot. I've spent the day trying to cultivate positive emotions - enjoying the exploration and the commitment, remembering to be patient, thinking back to all those miles in training.

But all this has been replaced by a creeping tide of defeat. I'm out of gas, going too slowly to make the 30-hour cut off. Even if the second 50 was possible, I wouldn't be quick enough. All I can do now is try and nurse my broken-down body home to Knockholt and throw in the towel...

6 UNCERTAINTY

You can see Botley Hill 15 miles to the north if you look out the windows at Hindleap Warren, the outdoor centre owned by London Youth, where I have my office.

For many of us, one of the most painful parts of the pandemic, has been Hindleap having to close to overnight visitors.

Hundreds of thousands of young people have come to the centre for a residential since it opened in the mid-60s. Taking part in teamwork activities, learning about environmental education in the middle of the woods and perhaps most importantly, getting an increasingly rarefied dose of adventure (26).

Many young people from one of the youth clubs affiliated to London Youth, make their first trip out of town to visit Hindleap, get their first glimpse of a wild animal or the Milky Way while they're there.

Like many in the industry, my friend Tony who runs the place, can't keep a quiet intensity out of his voice when he says the word 'adventure.' If I ask him what it means, he'll say 'it's about uncertainty, not knowing if you're going to make it.'

Before I became a fundraiser for London Youth, I was

an instructor at Hindleap, and early on in those days, Tony took me round Quarry Dene, one of the old stone mines under the North Downs, just up from Rockshaw Road. An initiation rite before leading a group of kids on a mining session down there.

Professionally clad in boiler suit and yellow wellies, balanced on the grassy verge, Tony is explaining the origin of the North Downs, using a makeshift model made from four or five layers of foam mat stuck together.

He gestures to the top layer:

'The chalk is actually the fossilised remains of tiny plankton, deposited on the floor of a shallow sea in the Cretaceous era, 75 million years ago...'

He bends the layers upwards in the middle

'...around the same time the Alps were created, tectonic pressure folded all the strata, including the chalk, up into a giant dome...'

With a flourish, he removes a central section of the model leaving a couple of layers in the centre, with all the bits of mat still intact at either end:

'...over millions of years, erosion has worn away the softer rock across the Weald, leaving the steeper chalky edges, the escarpments of the North and South Downs exposed...'

Lecture duly completed, we head down into the mine, where there are some spacious, pleasant exploratory passages. The mood becomes altogether more serious, when we reach the start of 'The Long Crawl', a much narrower section shaped like a stretched out letterbox. The roof lowers dramatically, forcing those who take on the challenge to crawl through the 30-40 foot slot 'commando style', using knees and elbows to achieve forward motion.

Tony goes first, his headlamp making its way methodically into the middle distance, leaving me more and more alone in the dark. Eventually there's the far away, slightly muffled shout of 'Ok! Come on through.' Then I have to summon the will to do it myself, to leave the relative safety of the larger chamber I'm in and venture into the unknown. And soon I'm experiencing the anxious feeling that continuing might be easier than turning back - twisting my neck so my helmet won't hit the ceiling, trying not to think about the claustrophobia and the weight of rock above my head, eventually figuring out the crab-like sequence of moves that is most efficient.

I tried to bottle that feeling and remember what it felt like when I encountered any young person unsure if they were going to make it, trying to find courage on the adventurous activities Hindleap ran. Because I knew from experience that sometimes when we're in doubt, another person can help us past the sticking point.

My first proper job had been as an instructor at an outdoor centre in the Shropshire Hills. Actually 'not a proper job' if you went with my Dad's take on things. It was the spring of 1992 and despite being a Cambridge graduate I was only earning £40 a week. But it didn't take me long to realise I was having the time of my life, paid to spend every day outdoors, maybe making a difference for some of the young people. The Sun Inn along the road looked after us in the evening, in exchange for most of our wages. Whenever a group left, we used to get in line and high kick in unison to the 'Meet the Gang' song. And Crowded House played on the radio most days, telling us 'always take the weather with you'.

My abiding memory from that first season – being clipped in at the top of the abseil tree, trying to help those who were most scared.

One girl was physically shaking when she arrived, a haunted look in her eyes, grabbing hold of the tree for dear life.

But she'd got that far, managed to make it up the rope ladder and scramble onto the platform. I reckoned she had a better than fifty-fifty chance of continuing.

I encouraged her to take some deep breaths. When she

was calmer and seemed ready, I talked about how strong the safety rope was, how her harness was fitted really securely, and how abseiling was actually one of the safest things she could do.

A minute or two later, still holding onto the tree, she was ready to show me she could stand with her feet shoulder width apart. And then as I carried on talking with a calm voice and kept the rope tight, I encouraged her to move to the edge of the platform and facing me, stand with her feet shoulder width apart again.

'It's ok. Take your time.'

After a few moments, she had a steelier look in her eye and was ready to go. She had found the will and as we looked at each other she started leaning backwards into the void. And then she was past the point of no return...

'Move your hand away from the figure of eight. Relax your grip with your right hand. Let the rope slide through.'

I watched as she felt what to do and adjusted her body into the right position. A minute or so later she was lowering herself the final few feet to the floor, and I was calling out her name to say well done.

It felt good to believe I'd played a small part as she found the confidence to overcome her uncertainty. And despite Dad's protestations, I was increasingly sure I'd chosen the right career - learning through adventure had a power I wanted to know more about.

7 KNOCKHOLT

I'm sat slumped on a chair inside Knockholt Village Hall. I've got my face mask on. Somehow my watch has stayed in race mode, telling me just over 12 hours have elapsed since I left the start line in Farnham. And it's still counting…

The number 278 remains symbolically pinned to my shorts. Dan, the guy on the door, didn't find my request to DNF convincing enough and sent me inside to regroup.

Now I'm trying again, explaining to Lesley the volunteer stood on the stage with the drop bags, why I'm not able to continue.

'I'm completely out of fuel. I haven't been able to eat anything. I'm utterly wiped out.'

'Well try and eat something now. You've got time. You're still a good two hours ahead of the cut off.'

I guess there's some logic in what she says. Even the prospect of walking to the station seems impossible in the state I'm in.

There's a guy sat to my right, not saying anything, looking similarly broken.

I have a breather and think about what I might be able to keep down. It's quiet in here and I don't feel so rushed.

At all the other aid stations up to now, I never felt able to settle enough to digest some food. I always felt pressure to get a move on, the weight of people in the queue behind.

My phone vibrates. It's Liz responding to my 'I'm completely wiped' message. She and Lee are telling me to try and eat something. Ian said this too when I phoned him before, calmly taking in the distress in my voice and not pushing too hard, but seeding the idea there might be another option. He'd radiated empathy and told me whatever I decided would be ok.

I wander over to one of the trestle tables, pour myself a cup of coke, perch back on my chair, sip it for a bit, then start taking thirsty gulps.

I go back up for a packet of ready salted crisps. Eat them one at a time, my tongue reaching out hungrily for the salt. I chew each mouthful carefully. Then pull out the foil-wrapped sausage roll from my bag and start munching on it.

Outside I can hear another guy loudly announcing to Dan –

'I want to drop from the race'

'You're sure?'

'I've never been surer about anything in my whole life!'

'Ok give me your number.'

See. I mutter to myself. That's how you do it.

Somewhere deep down, I'm pleased I hadn't been that assertive. I spent my whole life wanting to be more assertive. Maybe I shouldn't be worrying about that sort of thing any more…

There are loud noises coming from my stomach but thankfully they're about time, what were you thinking, grateful noises, rather than anything more ominous. Giving the food a chance to go down seems to be doing the trick.

Lesley is talking again as I start eating some Genoa fruit cake.

'Of course, it is a three or four mile walk to the station.

You realise it's not in the village...'

She's smiling mischievously as she says this, parading up and down the stage a bit. We both know what she's doing. I deployed this sort of sleight of hand enough times up the abseil tree.

I stay silent, a smile not very far away. I'm messing around with my pack, pulling out debris that's accumulated during the day. My drop bag is alongside – she fetched it for me. Actually, it might be nice to change my socks.

I luxuriate in undoing my laces, releasing the downward pressure from the tongues of my trainers. There's a sound like a hiss as I heave them off, then slowly lever off the grime coloured layers – almost glued on – and give my toes a wriggle before sliding the new socks carefully into place.

There's another top in my drop bag - might as well put it on in the loos. Wander round there. Strip off. Splash fast running cold water on my sweat-caked sunburnt face. Watch the grime from the afternoon swirl around the chipped enamel basin, then disappear down the plughole and into the darkness. Then pull on the laundered and comfy top.

Back in the hall Lesley is at it again.

'You're got three hours to get to Wrotham. That's plenty of time. You can walk that. They're nicer than us there as well. Much nicer.'

Keri, the guy to my right, is pulling on his pack and heading off.

There's not a single moment of me changing my mind. It's been a gradual shift over the last 40 minutes. I've so needed a proper sit down. They've kept offering me the chance to move outside to one of the chairs 'in the fresh air' but I haven't had the energy to shift my stuff from the spot where I first positioned myself.

My body has been crying out for food and drink, and the blood sugar flooding round my system, seeping into my brain, is literally turning the lights back on again.

Dan's experienced, nicely-judged intervention set in motion an alternative to a messy DNF. Ian, and Liz, and Lee have all been in my corner too. As has another volunteer giving me up to date info on precisely how much time I'm ahead of the cut off – which incidentally is 14 hours 40 minutes at Knockholt, not 14 hours flat as I thought.

But it's Lesley that has made the difference. Sometimes the chemistry with another person works - someone says the right thing at the right time and changes stuff. As well as being on the money with advice, she's been funny and light-hearted, and taken all the heaviness and heat out of the situation.

Don't commit to the whole of the second half. The 53 miles to Ashford through the night are too much to think about all at once. Just try and get to Wrotham. You can have a go at that.

8 ONLY LOVE

Since starting to work from home, I've developed a new routine. At eight o'clock on the dot every weekday morning I do a daily mile - round a lap Ilaria used to like.

If I'm lucky Pushkin, Paul and Annelly's cat, will wander down from Albert Road and wish me well. He's old and aimable and happy for me to imagine him as my friend. We have a tactile moment together, a triggering of pheromones, then because the clock is ticking, and I want to start work by half past eight, I bring the encounter to a close.

There may be a further interruption if Jasper, Alexandra Road's resident black and white feline madman, deigns to put in an appearance. He and Lily used to be friends – she always seemed to calm him down a bit. He might chew the dangling lead of my headphones for a second or two. Then suddenly break off to veer rapidly under a parked car and up into a nearby bush to scare of all the birds - previously hanging out peacefully there. Silently applauding his nimble-footedness, I might then be able to start my walk.

I cross over Framfield Road by The Alma, noticing all the new '2 Metres Apart' and 'One Way' signs, the shiny yellow and black tape strung along outside, the hint of stale ale on the air. I'm into a rhythm now, and a rickety fence, a row of broad beans, signal the start of the allotment. I'm listening to 'Stronger' the song in Rob Cowlin's video (27), zoning in on the North Downs Way. It's early July and swinging round and up the road by the Community Hospital, the first few blackberries are showing along the hedge.

I pass through the gate into the field, my new happy place, all long grass and sweeping views. It's not got long left, due to be bulldozed, turned into new houses in the next few months. Everything seems to be in doubt at the moment. But today I'm not going to let that get me down. I'm taking my place in this communal space, admiring the cloudless blue sky over Bird-in-Eye Hill and losing myself in the music. This is my unadulterated, immerse myself in the race time – twenty minutes to indulge my single-mindedness, narrow my focus and hunt out props from previous experience that might help me out, give me traction if I'm up against it.

I remember watching an RSC production of The Tempest, Prospero centre stage, arms wide, eyes to the heavens – channelling everything he had to summon up the storm. I think about the trapped emotions of the lockdown, the loneliness, the hours of effort in training, and imagine I too can channel that into this single aim, leaving it all out on the route, using every drop of my physical and spiritual self, everything I've ever learnt, to find a way to endure.

Fanciful, I guess. But it still gives me goose bumps.

It's good to have a goal, to set my heart on something.

Or is it? Others have warned me about my obsessive streak before. I had a mate at university who used to be very disparaging when I got too intense. Paolo my Italian therapist friend, had also quite sensibly flagged the danger of investing everything in one activity, explained how putting all your chips on one square, leaves you horribly vulnerable psychologically if things don't work out. And not long before he died, my Dad had infamously told me 'don't get too obsessed with this running business Gruff!' – sussing out I was taking it all a bit too seriously.

It's too late now! Needing some reassurance, I look up the Theodore Roosevelt quote on my phone

'It is not the critic who counts; not the man who points out how the strong man stumbles, or where the doer of deeds could have done them better. The credit belongs to the man who is actually in the arena, whose face is marred by dust and sweat and blood; who strives valiantly; who errs, and comes short again and again, because there is no effort without error and shortcoming; but who does actually strive to do the deeds; who knows the great enthusiasms, the great devotions; who spends himself in a worthy cause; who at the best knows in the end the triumph of high achievement, and who at the worst, if he fails, at least fails while daring greatly...' (28)

Shaggy is up next on the playlist – 'Only Love' my favourite song for this time of day. The lyrics loosen me up, making me exuberant and full of hope. I'm heading along Selby Close now, speeding up as I make for home, imagining how good it will be to have all the hills behind me, adrenaline flushing away the tiredness, the road into Ashford stretching out ahead.

9 SPENCERVILLE

Out the back of the hall, Lesley is supposedly having a break. She's had to keep her facemask on inside, all the volunteers have. But she's happy to point me in the direction of the marker tape, the race route Centurion signs.

Walking through the rest of the village, I feel like I can legitimately hold my head high again, that it's actually ok to lap up the odd smattering of applause, the one very English and understated 'well done' that comes my way.

Striding up the lane, I'm happy living from moment to moment, relieved to still be in the race. Aware of my surroundings again, I realise we're properly over the north side of the ridge, down the dip slope of the chalk for the first time.

The harsh, dismissive voice that was in such control an hour ago has gone, replaced by a gentler, on-my-side sort of voice.

'You did a brave thing back there son. Well done. You've got this.'

I'm not sure why but I find myself welling up.

'Everything's going to be ok. You're just a bit emotional that's all.'

There's a tingling feeling up and down the back of my neck, salty tears running down my face. These are combining into a renewed and very powerful sense of purpose. A surge of adrenaline, that feels like a forcefield, is carrying me up the hill.

Ok focus. Settle down. I talked with Louise about being 'Creative' in the third quarter of the race, being prepared to make it up as I go along. Let's give that a try. I left half-way exactly two hours inside the cut-off time. And Lesley said I had three hours to get to Wrotham. Simple, don't take more than that - keep your time cushion, you might end up needing it later.

Soon I'm back on the crest, 700 foot up, the Weald spread out below, disappearing into the heatwave, and over to the left, the long line of the Downs ending in a slope down to the Darent Valley.

I pull alongside another runner. She's debating whether to open her packet of crisps. I tell her this bit's joggable and encourage her to come with me anyway. She laughs and saves them for later. Her name is Bozena and we spend a companionable mile together, trundling down the zig-zags on the 450-foot descent back to the bottom again.

I can feel the calories from half-way kicking in and encouraged by our 11-minute mile down the hill, press on over the M25 bridge and manage a longer spell of running. Chugging through a little housing estate I spot a familiar looking figure on the left – it's Spencer, self-styled 'elite jogger'. Did he ever get hold of Kerry's Hale Lane cheesecake I wonder? He's beaming from ear to ear, taking a photo of me on his phone, as I blurt out -

'I nearly gave up at Knockholt!'

'Keep going boy! You've got a book to write!'

I'm buzzing and he spurs me on into Otford. I cross over the Darent, river number three on the trip. Somewhere here, Edmund Ironside fought a battle with the Danes during his ill-fated few months as King of the English (29). A few decades later, none of this tribal squabbling mattered any more as William the Conqueror rocked up and settled things once and for all.

Checks notes Otford was strategically important for centuries of course – the place where the 'Old Road' along the Downs to the Channel met the route down the Darent from London. Exactly five hundred years ago, Henry the Eighth and Catherine of Aragon famously stayed in the Archbishop's Palace in Otford on their way along to the continent for a summit with the French King. Owing to not much of significance being discussed, and ostentatious, by the sounds of it fairly untasteful, displays of wealth on both sides, this meeting later became known as 'The Field of the Cloth of Gold' (30).

To be honest I'm not worrying about any of this. I'm soon busy renaming Otford - 'Spencerville.' Ten minutes after the first sighting I do a double take as he's there again sat outside a pub in the centre of the town. Afterwards, it turns out he was omnipresent throughout the whole race, also making his way to Bluebell Hill to take over from Helen on pacing duties for Ally Whitlock, helping her to an eventual, brilliant 48th place (31).

The temperature hasn't dropped at all, and the effort and adrenaline of the last few miles has taken its toll. I slow up, losing my sense of humour just as the gradient begins to kick in again. By Otford Station, the crews are spread out along the side of the road, another reminder I could have been better prepared and set this up for myself. These aid points have often been positioned just before the major hills, giving runners a reboot when needed most. I try not to look envious as I struggle by and one lady in a little alcove takes pity on me.

'Are you alright? Have you got everything you need? Do you want anything to eat?'

I thought I was done crying three quarters of an hour ago...

'Have you got any ice?' I ask

She reaches into a cool box and hands me nearly half a

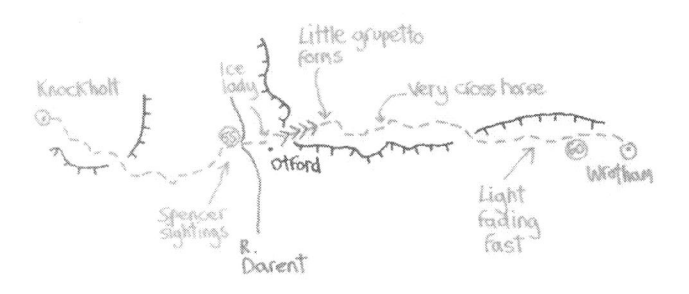

[Hand-drawn map sketch showing: Knockholt, Ice lady, Little gruppetto forms, Very cross horse, Otford, Spencer sightings, R. Darent, Light fading fast, Wrotham]

bag. She might as well be giving me a wad of banknotes.

'Are you sure? Have you got enough for your runner?

She points to another full bag in the box, and several profuse thank yous later, encourages me on my way. Her random act of kindness gives the world an intense positive sheen and spurs me on again.

Hands on knees, I make my way up the 450 feet of sadistic steps out of Otford. The ice is balanced on the back of my neck, making the effort just about bearable.

Other runners are up ahead now. Some sixth sense tells me I mustn't let them go. Blinking to try and stop the sweat stinging my eyes, I can't judge the distance, and yet, slowly but surely, they seem to be getting closer as I grind up the climb.

Over the top of the hill, the junction is made, and we form a little gruppetto. There are two women deep in conversation who appear to be nailing it. As I try to stay with them, I admire from a few yards behind, their apparently effortless blend of speed walking and easy jogging. Another much younger guy does the same. Our little group pulls together for a while.

It's a beautiful sultry evening, the clouds infused with rose and gold. There's a sudden moment of drama as, with a wild look in his eye, a horse occupies the path. He's sweating and sulky - pissed at being repeatedly disturbed. Even though we arc round at a very respectful distance, he's still threatening to kick off. I can see where he's coming from...

By the time we make our way off the far end of the Downs, the light is fading fast and care is needed on a short rutted section of path through the woods. There's an unspoken, probably not very sensible, push to get to Wrotham before pulling headtorches out. Based on what my watch says, and not having studied the map for a while, I half hoped the aid station would be here at the bottom of the hill. No, there's still a long mile and a half following an ancient lane in the gathering gloom. The group separates out again as our collective blood sugar drops and we all retreat into the tunnel vision of individual effort.

It's pitch black by the time civilisation finally materialises. I blunder around in the dark making a couple of wrong turns, then, more by luck than judgement, stumble blinkingly on the bustle and bright lights of the aid station at Wrotham Village Hall.

10 BROKEN

Masked up, I'm sat on a high-speed train whizzing through the Kent countryside, looking out the window as summer flashes by. Like most travellers heading this way, we're being funnelled north-west along the Vale of Holmesdale, M20 to the left, North Downs to the right (32).

Here's Hollingbourne already, scene of my 90s summer job in the stores with Costain, helping them build the new motorway. In a blink or two it's astern and a few minutes later we're starting to slow down, crossing the Medway and pulling into a largely deserted Ebbsfleet. Time to change trains...

It's day one of my holiday and I'm ticking off a lot of firsts. First drive out the area, first time on public transport, first takeaway coffee since lockdown. This requires a certain mental dexterity after months of caution, months of putting life on hold. But needs must - the race is four weeks today and I've got my running gear on, the last 30 miles of the route to recce.

I head out of Rochester Station and into town, trying to find the North Downs Way. Turning left by Medway Council Registry Office, the small print about births and deaths brings to mind an exhausting afternoon in Norwich a few years before, me and Ian doing the paperwork after Dad died...

Along past the keep and the Castle, last spotted in 1979, a school trip in Miss Cronin's class.

Now here's Kings Rochester – the boarding school Uncle Bernard was packed away to in the late 50s – often discussed in my family as he and Dad were orphaned early - it meant the younger of the two brothers was looked after. Now I'm seeing it for the first time and reimagining that era afresh.

It's quiet along Borstal Road, the Edwardian houses more affluent than most of the Medway towns. The sun glints off the river and the low hills on the far side give the scene an English riviera feel. Feeling suddenly hot, I stop on the spur of the moment to buy another bottle of water.

Stood on the bridge, I'm trying to imagine being here exhausted in the middle of the night, traffic speeding by on the M2. Past racers have reported the crossing as a pivotal part of the journey, as well as getting a little freaked out by the Samaritan signs along the walkway. There is a whiff of Scandi noir about it all. Saga in her mustard-coloured Porsche wouldn't be out of place.

Enough procrastination, time to actually start running, begin the climb up to Bluebell Hill, one of the highest parts of the course, and bugger it I'm lost already. Should I really be needing to climb this gate with barbed wire all over it?

An unlikely saviour emerges out of the haze. He has the easy practiced lope, the paraphernalia of a seasoned ultrarunner. He looks uncannily like Ivor Hewitt. He is Ivor Hewitt! Prepping for the race too, and grinning, he points out the right turn I should have taken back down along the hedge. Given his general air of competence it's sensible for him to head off in front of me.

Although I manage to run the three miles up to the top, he's long gone by the time I get there. Slightly disorientated at a car park someone points out the path -

'there was a bloke ahead of you – he went that way.'

Plummeting back down the hill, alongside the A229, I remember all those Sundays driving up here to see Gran and Grandad - then just Gran. Did she have to go to the registry office all by herself to have his death recorded?

Past the sign for the Neolithic burial chamber at Kit's Coty and the path soon leads to the foot of another climb up through Westfield Wood. Here the idea I might be fit enough to run these hills is quickly dismissed. These steps are my first experience of a full-on North Downs hands-on-knees job as they rise 350 feet in half a mile. Come to think of it, Mum and Dad's wedding was in Chatham, in her childhood church - their marriage was under Medway jurisdiction, that must have been recorded there too…

I'm soon running again along the crest, picking my way along a ploughed field, then passing a cadre of soldiers, heavily packed, out on a training exercise. Mum and Dad only met because Uncle Bernard went to Kings, Dad wouldn't have developed ties down here otherwise, I wouldn't have…

Down a stony chute into Detling, over the main road we used to take up to the Kent County Show. Climbing once more, I spy the elusive Mr Hewitt, disappearing into a wood, soon gone for good. Up top I get lost again, assuming the North Downs Way would carry on along the crest rather than head straight back down. When I do rediscover the proper path, it develops a wild side. Set after set of up and down steps are bordering on the malign to be honest. Is it my imagination or is it malevolent to seek out so many hills? Did nobody know about contouring?!

Fiddling around with my new watch I programmed this route in, with an ambitious estimated pace of 10 minutes 15 seconds per mile. Now the watch seems keen to let me know I'm falling further and further behind my target time.

Eventually I'm down at Hollingbourne and here 15

miles into the run, the elevation levels off to a more manageable level. Seven, eight, nine more miles go by relatively uneventfully. Then I feel a niggle in my right shin. An uncomfortableness I haven't experienced before. Not there... then there... a bit like a conjuring trick.

Luckily there's a distraction to take my mind of it - I've run out of water. It's been quite hot and with all the hills two litres was nowhere enough. Now I'm searching for some sort of mercy mission outdoor tap. Nope! There isn't one anywhere through here - you'll just have to be thirsty.

Time to take my mind off the mounting issues with an unscheduled stop, some impromptu poppy photography. Setting off again, my right shin has seized up completely and it's pulsing with pain, almost impossible to run on. I have to try though, there are still four miles to go.

Soldiering on, I'm helped for a mile or two running with Geoff, a local guy who's doing the 100 too, who points me in the direction of the stadium in Ashford. Although completely out of my way, I've decided I need to get to the stadium to complete the 30 miles.

Once I'm done, I'm parched and desperate for a drink. Now there's just the mile and half of limping back to where the car's parked by the station. It takes over an hour. And of course, there's no shop or garage in this part of Ashford. Was it really necessary to go all the way to the stadium, to create this extra suffering? Don't answer that! After the afternoon's efforts it feels like someone wearing steel toe-caps has kicked me on the shinbone as hard as they can...

By the time I crawl in through my front door a few hours later I'm completely lame, a broken man. It's a case of North Downs One – Gareth Nil. I'll need a miracle to make the race at this rate.

11 THE MEDWAY GAP

Lesley's trick to get me out of Knockholt worked, encouraging me to build a head of steam. Now I'm safely ensconced here at Wrotham, pulling out the race no longer seems like an option. I'll just pick up what I need and set off again.

But the effort of the last few hours has taken its toll, and my body clock thinks it's time for bed. I faff around spilling water on the floor, having a cup of coke which disagrees with me, trying another unsuccessful toilet stop. Then I set off without my pole, forgetting to say thank you. I go back and remember both, getting the feeling the volunteers have seen a lot of this sort of cloth-headedness in the last few hours.

Back out in the dark, I spot two familiar figure ahead and run down a little hill to join them. They're ok with me tagging along again. We do the introductions properly this time. Zoe's done a lot of 100s before and I remember chatting to her picking up the tracker at the start. She's seems to be going really well. Jane explains she isn't taking part in the race, she's Zoe's pacer. And also, in other news, Race Director for the Arc of Attrition winter 100 along the Cornish coast (33). Do I fancy it?! I'll have a think! Jane also lets on she has a bone to pick with the North Downs after leaving Botley Hill in an ambulance, for heatstroke related reasons a few years before.

We take it in turns to lead, back up the hill and into a long stretch of woodland, alternate running and walking. They seem really on it and strangely for me, the running's the straightforward part - Jane's power walking so fast it's hard to keep up.

There's a discussion on leading lights of the sport and how nice they all are, then wondering what's happening up ahead of us, Jane checks her phone and announces Peter Windross the frontrunner has dropped out at Detling. Sobering news - if he's struggling…

There's a sudden, easy to miss right turn then a stony, stepped descent, lined with yew trees, spooky in the torchlight. We slow up as it steepens towards the bottom. Then we're on the familiar lower trackway again, marked Pilgrim's Way on the map, which also shows a 'Long Barrow' (34) just below us in the dark....

The valley narrows, the lights of Bluebell Hill in touching distance across the far side. Although it's only about six miles over there, it'll take us more like 14 or 15. We're doing a big loop up to the north to cross the river at Rochester. Speaking of which, there are the lights of the M2 bridge in the distance. Knowing the ground from the bridge to the end, and fighting tiredness, the crossing is now my number one focus. I'm ticking off the miles in my head desperate for it to get closer.

The moon rises, blood red in the tropical air. I dig in on the rise to Holly Hill and suddenly Jane and Zoe aren't there anymore. I look for them in the aid station queue, and while I fill my water bottles, but they don't arrive. A nearby fluorescent skeleton spookily warns 'Beware the Chair'. Heeding his advice, I head off, back on my mission to make the bridge.

Afterwards I find out Zoe's race went downhill a few miles further on. She was suddenly violently sick and dizzy and not able to walk or see straight. After 90 minutes in the back of an ambulance, she begged to be let out, then, with Jane by her side, made a Herculean effort to make it up 500-foot Bluebell Hill ahead of the cut off. She missed it by a few minutes but went down fighting, head high.

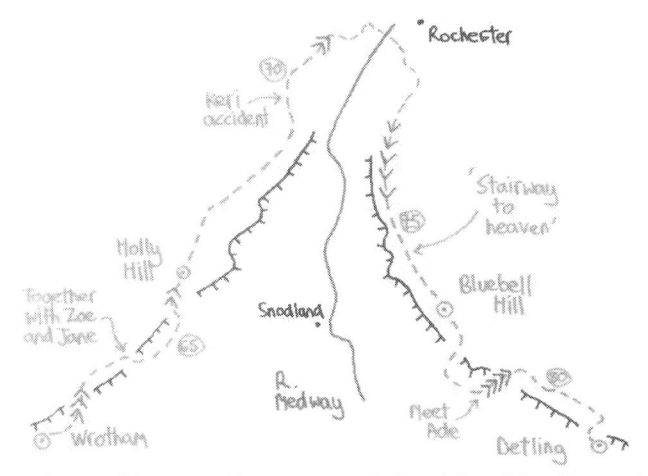

Meanwhile back in the woods there's a familiar looking figure ahead. It's Keri, the guy sat next to me at Knockholt. We move together through the trees, watching for roots. He's got a fast walking rhythm with click-clack double poles. We've been going nearly 18 hours. There's a communal vibe and we're both focused so there's not much small talk.

A guy comes speeding past with a see-you-later running style. I'm worried about time, fixated on making the end of the Medway Bridge by 01.00. Bitter experience has shown what the last 30 miles are like. I might only manage three miles an hour, especially if it's hot again tomorrow, and I'm running on empty. And this would still give me an hour's cushion ahead of my cut off at 12.00. I'm feeling relatively fresh right now. I can run some of these downhills.

I tell Keri I'm going to jog a bit. He's worried about time too and sticks with me. A mile or so later he goes over violently on his ankle. He's in agony, but carries on with gritted teeth, trying to maintain cut off pace. After 10 minutes of despairing effort, it's clearly all in vain, and gutted he announces, 'I'm not going to make it'. I stay with him until the road where he phones the Race Doctor and his race - and dream of doing all four 100 milers in a year - comes to a premature end. Despite the injury, Keri shows his dedication by volunteering at the Thames Path 100 a few weeks later…

Try not to blame yourself. Focus on this next climb. Voices in the distance behind you. Don't let them catch up. Keep on it. Run when you can. Now blink at being suddenly ejected out of the dark, into an amber-lit middle-of-the-night modern world. Walkways, underpasses spray-painted with tags, scraps of Centurion marker tape dancing in the wind. Back in the day, some urban planning whizz figured out how to thread bewildered foot-folk like me past Rochester's main arterial road, over the M2, and safe from thundering juggernauts, through to the far side of the Medway Bridge.

My sister's 6,000 miles away in Hong Kong, watching my dot, knowing the bridge is a landmark. Allow yourself a quick selfie to send her later. Then snap out of it as a no-lights petrolhead comes whizzing by on his bike doing about 70.

You've made the south end by one am. Well done. Now press on up Bluebell Hill, stay at this doable three miles an hour. Your feet are hurting, your legs are sore, your single pole is working away. You're on a kind of stairway to heaven, and the track will always be climbing away into the darkness…

Eventually, after several lifetimes, here's the aid station appearing round a corner like an apparition - the Centurion banners and the reassuring bleep-bleep of the chip timer. No, you're not dreaming. Use the music playing in the background to wake you up for the two am

Covid protocols. Sanitise your hands, fill your bottles for the leg to Detling, now go and sit in an isolated camping chair and chomp your banana. All around are silent shapes sat with hooded heads trying to dredge up remaining dregs of willpower. Out beyond the circle of chairs, a worryingly horizontal figure is quietly beseeching the guy in charge to be allowed to stay lying down for 10 minutes.

Don't get comfortable. It's time to head off... And oh bugger what's that feeling? Ok stop and vomit by the side of the path, and now retch a few more times. Are you done? The banana was a bad idea then! Try a drink. Good you can still drink water. You haven't died. Water will have to do.

Toughen up. Get on with it. Run downhill for the next mile, watch for the hidden right turn and the steps. Jog through the trippy Blakes Seven underpass.

After these couple of hours alone, there's suddenly a figure on the right speaking to someone on the phone. He hangs up and asks to tag along. Tells me he won't hold me up. He's built like an Olympic rower. I say yes. The full on climb up through Westfield Wood acts as an icebreaker. Then we string together some joint running efforts along the top. The wind's picked up and there's a storm brewing over Faversham way. Jane did say something about it raining in Ashford. Time for some introductions. He's Ade an architect; I'm Gareth a fundraiser for London Youth. And we're both completely fucked. Looking back over the lowlights of the last 20 hours or so, we vow this will be our last 100 mile race – it is needless suffering and pain.

And on that note, in his research, Derek Bright points out that in the Middle Ages, 'pilgrimage was used by both ecclesiastical and secular courts as a form of punishment' (35). Wrongdoers were sent along here to atone for their misdemeanours. This never-ending push through the night has been punishing alright.

Mile 82. Ade asking me again, as the person with the

local knowledge, where the next aid station is? He's exuded calm since I met him, but this question is becoming urgent for both of us. Soon, I hope, very soon. Yes, I know I said that before. He distracts himself talking about all the food he's going to eat when we get there.

Finally, here's the right turn and the awkward descent down into Detling. Despite everything I can't stop myself from running it and Ade shouts 'you go on'.

Although I wouldn't see him again, I hadn't jinxed Ade and he did make it to the finish ok. In fact, Ade was a bit of a dark horse on the 'this will be my last 100 miler' front. He was picking up a Thames Path buckle four weeks later...

12 'AN ENTRY FEE'

The first week of my holiday – lying on the couch with an elevated leg – isn't going well. There won't be any more recces of the route. Activities include icing my shin, googling sports injury sites to figure out what's wrong and trying to stop seeing the North Downs as some sort of malevolent adversary. Surely, it's superstitious nonsense to think like that…

Setting off complacently to do the Icknield Way, Rob Macfarlane had a spectacular, painful bike crash on his first day on the chalk. Afterwards his friend was unsurprised and told him 'this was an entry fee to the old ways… now you can proceed. You're in… you've paid your due.'

If the lesson is that a certain amount of respect, a calmer mindset, is required for journeying, I've learnt it. Or at least I think I have!

In the days immediately after the recce, a multi-coloured bruise spreads purposefully across my lower leg and there's acute pain coming from my right shin. I've got ample time for worrying and soon convince myself it's a stress fracture.

Chris is one of those being sympathetic on social media. He's also lined up for the North Downs 100 but has injury problems too - a torn ligament in his ankle. Eventually I follow his advice and get my shin checked out at the Community Hospital. The nurse reckons it's only a swollen tendon and is reluctant to order an x-ray – even if it was a stress fracture it probably wouldn't show up this early on. More ice and rest required.

After seven days of climbing the walls, enough is enough. I've booked somewhere in the Lakes for the second week and I'll be going up there come what may.

Jim, the owner at Lowthwaite B&B (36), shows me round from a safe distance and wearing one of those plastic face shields, explains all the Covid protocols. He's empathetic about my shin and doesn't warn me off heading up Little Mell Fell as soon as I arrive. The house is in the middle of nowhere and there's very few people around - a delight to soak up mountain air for the first time in nearly a year. Picking my way carefully down off the hill, about a mile and a half into the walk, my shin starts complaining bitterly. Well you knew that was going to happen!

Next day I'm being sensible, and for the first time in pretty much ever, not going up anything. I do a walking loop round Gowbarrow Fell. Completing the 8 mile circuit - with a short section of test-it-out jogging above Ullswater – means things are definitely looking better... Until I get out the car in Penrith and the short walk to the chippy is agony. Back at the B&B Jim's got my icepack ready.

Tuesday. You shouldn't be here at the head of Haweswater with so many tempting fells in the vicinity. Guess you can always turn around if the shin gets too sore. Halfway up Gatescarth Pass it is too sore. Time to discover rehabilitation treatment phase two – dunking it in a soothing, icy stream for 20 minutes. Elemental my dear Watson! That's better. Now slowly amble to the top of Harter Fell.

And here at the sultry back end of the afternoon,

although you entered the how much height can you climb in a week Centurion 'One Up Challenge' weeks ago, you're definitely not taking part. No, you're only heading round to High Street because it's the logical way to complete the circuit, not because you want to get to 4,000 feet for the day.

Wednesday. Up and down Blencathra in the rain. Feel it pitter-patter harder on your waterproof each time you get higher into the cloud. Another 4,000 feet. Call it a day at lunch due to the throbbing shin.

A pattern is emerging. Take the shin to the limit, let the pain tell you to stop. Then give it some rest and go again. Laura – once my pacer, now as a trainee physiotherapist my informal injury advisor – confirms this isn't totally nuts. Swollen tendons don't mind getting angry apparently.

Thursday. What was that about a calmer mindset? March up Helvellyn from Thirlmere as fast as you can, don't worry about making a noise like a steam train. Do it within the hour, then drop down and go again. Chalk up 7,000 feet of climbing by the end of the day and 18,000 for the week - Mont Blanc on the One Up scoreboard.

I like Jim. Not only does he and his wife do wonderful socially-distanced breakfasts, he's somehow keeping the business going despite everything, and doesn't mind giving me the icepack from his freezer every night. He knows about the race and understands what I need to do. Try and recover, but at the same time give the shin as much shock therapy as it can handle – so it's ready for the onslaught in two and a half weeks' time.

Friday. Back up Helvellyn like it's your day job, pick up the highway along the ridge then roll down the zigzags to Grisedale Tarn. Turn left up towards Saint Sunday and concentrate on where you put your feet on this exposed climb to the col – which feels quite alpine in places. And enjoy this beautiful day in the mountains – bright sunshine, crystal clear air quality, all the summits in touching distance. You shouldn't be trying to bag the remaining height to get to Everest, but you can't help yourself. It's ok son, you're hooked on this sort of thing!

Next up, Fairfield from the Tarn. Dig in for the effort. It's steep so pace yourself. Give that woman on her way down enough room and be careful finding traction on this unstable pile of scree. Wait, who's this punter coming up fast in your peripheral vision? Have a look after the next turn. Ok here we go - young, looks like a player, fell runner type, gaining on me. No problem if he passes, no problem at all - make him work for it though. Move up a couple of gears. Good. Keep it at that, up near maximum heart rate. Don't worry if the sweat gets in your eyes. Here's the summit plateau and he hasn't come by yet. Try to keep your breathing steady as you pass him on the way back down!

Quick pit stop at the bottom to get some calories in. Here's that woman again – she has a calm, authoritative air – a Headmistress or something? Get up and go before she comes by you, but say something, this is the third time you've seen her today.

'No rest for the wicked!'

Ok good. Head up Seat Sandal, that'll give you another 500 feet or so.

Heading back down, my shin is starting to throb and seeing the woman for a fourth time we both decide to stop and talk. She's reveals she's been thinking about what I said. It resonated because she's always driving herself. But now she's thinking about pausing for breath more.

'Do we give ourselves enough rest, enough time to enjoy the mountains?' she asks no-one in particular, with the hint of a smile on her face.

I sheepishly let on about my plan to bag 10,000 feet today but that also my shin hurts. She doesn't tell me what to do and a few minutes later we go our separate ways.

Our chance meeting has an air of serendipity, seems to be part of the big picture. I'm now reconsidering this relentless need to push myself, to always be chasing the next goal. I have a different mindset as I pick my way back down to the tarn. I stop and give my shin a long soak in its cold purifying depths.

Later I head away from the crowded ridgeline and seek out Brownrigg Well – the spring below the summit of Helvellyn – to get more water. Once I've filled my bottles, it's nice to have a breather, allow myself some time off. This is a holiday after all. No-one else in sight, and out west there's just upland country, an unbroken line of mountain tops from left to right, a calm and serenity to the scene that's brought me back up here again and again. Beneath me the water bubbles softly as it comes out the fellside.

The race is 15 days away, my shin is getting better and my fitness is fine. There's no need to do any more climbing. I can stop now.

13 THE OLD ROAD

It's just before dawn as I leave Detling aid station. Inside the village hall it became apparent both Emma and Peter from Hindleap had messaged me during the middle of the night to send encouragement. They must have set the alarm to do that – it's hard not to be emotional about this degree of thoughtfulness... A shivery feeling brings me back to earth - water seems to have leaked out over my top and I can feel it more, out in the open air.

Then I start moving, heading along past the deserted cricket pitch, swinging left where the marker tape drapes, picking up the trail again. Negotiating the relatively civilised gradient of the first climb, objects are starting to become clear beyond the wavering beam of my headtorch, which won't be needed much longer.

The retreating darkness encourages me, brings on a let's-do-this frame of mind. I'm soon back on the crest of this unceasing wave of hills, marching along, buffeted and exhilarated by a tempestuous wind, gusting around me in a stormy, pewter and purple half-light. I finally have the whole place to myself, and there's alchemy in the air.

It feels good to be alive, in the here and now, in this ephemeral moment between night and day. Our decimated

[Hand-drawn map showing: Detling, Seven hills section, first signs of light, Views over Holmesdale, Hollingbourne, Stop to fix blister, Harrietsham, Lenham]

field has been tossed this way and that like flotsam. We've been thrown down into the abyss, pulled along the springline, then sucked back up with the buzzards again. Yet there's such an invigorating lifeforce in this struggle. It is all consuming. I've given it everything…

And for a second or two, in the midst of my effort… there's a here then gone… flicker of connection with those that travelled this way before.

Perhaps a 14th century merchant, thinking about filling his amulet, the phial round his neck with rejuvenating 'blood' from Becket's shrine, getting an early start, wanting to reach Canterbury before the end of the day (37).

Or an outrider for Henry II, ordered ahead from Boxley Abbey, on a similar early summer morning, route finding for the King, making his way to the Cathedral to pay penance for the Archbishop's murder four years before (38).

Maybe even a tribal representative, many millennia earlier, sent along 'The Old Road' to follow up on rumours that the flatter 'channel' of lower lying chalk, which had for generations been slowly inundating with water, was now completely flooded over, turning us into an island kingdom…(39)

Afterwards, reading Rob Macfarlane's rediscovery of 'The Old Ways', I realise it's been common for those navigating these long established paths across the soft white rock, to report some sort of morphing of time, and in the nineteenth century especially, 'a chalky mysticism established itself, a belief that it was a super-conductor of the sympathetic historical mind, allowing simultaneities and compassion to reach out across millennia.' (40)

Back in the race, I have nothing to fear anymore. I run the descents when I can and power carefully up the steps. I'm aware in the rutted and rocky runnel, avoid all the low hanging undergrowth and watch for the adverse camber. When the seventh steep hill in quick succession tries to underdo me, I say bring it on. This is the North Downs Way greatest hits section after all.

We're heading along the top for the final time, this vertical world at odds with the flatness of Holmesdale, stretching away into the ether on the right. I can see a little cluster of runners on a headland of chalk half a mile ahead. I'm soon there too, then not long after, tackling the steep, try not to accelerate out of control, descent into the valley.

I plonk down on the grass for a moment or two, nearly tipping over backwards. Sensible to stop and patch this blister on the ball of my foot. Done. Problem solved, time to get going again.

The single-track trail is over. Bring on the more sedentary Pilgrim's Way, the track I remember from growing up. Stride up the long drag out of Hollingbourne, run this little descent, then plough on up the other side.

And suddenly, sooner than expected, here's neatly set out Lenham aid station on a triangular patch of grass, the reassuring double bleep of the final chip timer. There's almost a party atmosphere, a sense the worst may be behind us. One volunteer tells us there's about a half marathon to go. Trying to keep a straight face I tell her, 'just the 90 minutes then!'

A top up of water, a cake bar, and off again, soon

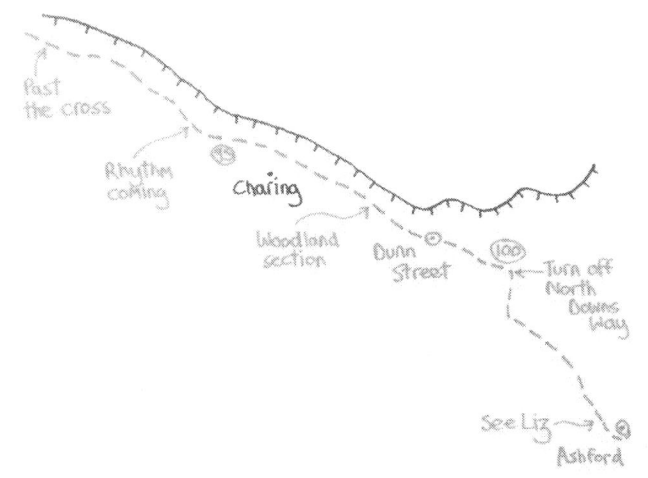

passing Swadelands where I went to school. And the Cross, scene of my very first cross-country, my brother and sisters too. They'll be watching my dot expecting it to be moving faster along here, for posterity you understand.

Sensing them nearby, I start to jog, get an inkling a new rhythm might establish itself. A young woman, out for a Sunday run, overtakes me. I let myself get carried along in her slipstream and pass another guy.

I'm punch drunk tired and pulling this from a deep well but I'm craving the finish now and manage one, two then three faster miles in a row. They're only 12 minute jobs but I'll take that. I'm pleased with my momentum, passing more people, crossing the main road in Charing, running down the lane, speed-marching up the hill at the end, jogging through the woods and here's the banner for Dunn Street already, the final aid station. There's no need to break my flow. The volunteer in the lane has already checked my number and I can go.

I run down through the final few fields, watching in semi-disbelief as my watch vibrates and dutifully flashes up the figures 12:05 and mile number 100. It's been an almost continuous, fifteen-hour effort, since Lesley pointed me on way yesterday evening.

I've never driven myself this hard in my whole life, never been this tired. Through the precariousness of the pandemic, the lay-off from the painful shin, the chaos of those last few miles before half-way, I never allowed the idea I might actually finish, to properly establish itself. Now the possibility is starting to sink in...

Here's the final right turn off the trail. Head into the churchyard. Keep a straight face as you say 'Farnham', when the man out for a Sunday stroll asks how far we've all come.

March up the hill. Start running down the other side. Now I'm on the outskirts of Ashford and turning right onto the main road near where my sister used to live. And here's Liz filming me on her phone. There's a pleasing confusion about seeing her, and the normality of our conversation brings a sense of returning to civilisation, like re-entering the earth's atmosphere after a moon mission. I gabble for a bit and she tells me to stop talking. The sun's coming out again and it's suddenly almost as hot as yesterday. Time to get this done.

Round the final roundabout, be careful crossing the main road. Down the long straight, over the railway bridge and then there's the sign for the left turn into the stadium. The hill down onto the track is bliss and then I'm on the rust-coloured surface itself.

I'm 51, I've been running my whole life, and I've never been on a proper track before. It has a wonderful give to it, a springiness I wasn't expecting. Hugging the inside rail, I start to accelerate around the final bend.

Those hairs on the back of my neck have been overworked by this experience. Surfing a wave of adrenaline and very close to crying with joy, I ignite the afterburners, surge past a couple of other runners in the finishing straight, and arms and legs pumping, sprint in across the line.

14 COLDRUM

Afterwards, all the talk is about the 'wrong' sort of records being broken (41). Even though my effort of 27 hours and 33 minutes would normally be in the bottom half, I end up 59th. And amongst the others, Ally and Andy and Geoff pulled off impressively fast times, Giacomo and Sonny kept their Grand Slam dreams alive, and Chris somehow finished too, despite his ankle injury.

But although 235 people started the race, only 107 got to the end. Many didn't make the cut offs because of the heat. I'm sad to hear neither Darren nor Rob reached Ashford, but they'll both put in very strong performances and get PBs at the Thames Path 100 in much nicer weather four weeks later.

Although I was quickly over my 'never again' conversation with Ade, the North Downs 100 had been more than enough for me for now.

There were a few pointers to its impact…

…Dozing in the car on the way home, then waking up and yelling in alarm at Liz, convinced she was driving at full speed into an ambulance parked across the middle of the road. Her telling me there was no ambulance.

…Weighing myself the day after and realising I'd lost

six kilos.

...Still feeling like I needed to be on an IV drip four days later.

But there was also a sense of renewal, like I'd been rebuilt somehow. As if the previous version of me was slowly and systematically destroyed in the first 50 miles, and some new sense of self emerged out of the push from Knockholt to the finish.

All of us involved that weekend got some insight into resilience – often cited these days as a character trait people should aspire to. I've spent most of my life wondering how on earth you're supposed to go about acquiring it. Perhaps by concentrating on uncertainty, its close cousin. Shrugging off being sick after Bluebell Hill, taking on all those steps after Detling, I did feel almost armour-plated. And this felt far removed from thinking I was at breaking point sat on the log at Botley Hill or running out of fuel on mile 48. But that second wind in the Sunday small hours, emerged out of the journey to get there - putting up with a great deal of disquiet for most of the race. Reading reports from other runners it became clear many of us had a pretty similar experience. Maybe it's when we endure through unease and insecurity that resilience starts to develop. And maybe this might provide a crumb of comfort, for living with, and through, the pandemic.

Tony's definition of adventure was met. I set off not knowing if I had what it takes. Last year, on the Thames, dozens of volunteers helped me, but this time, I wouldn't have made it without interventions from others. Dan and Lesley at Knockholt, the ice lady at Wrotham, and Zoe and Jane. These people, amongst others, made the difference between success and failure. I never meant to write another book about the race, but in the days and weeks after, I couldn't help myself. It was one way of saying thank you.

In the later stages of the Saturday afternoon heat

exhaustion and hunger had shut down much of my sensory awareness. Many aspects of what happened, impressions from within the white heat of the experience, were in danger of being lost for good. And in trying to piece together what unfolded, I also found myself getting engrossed in the stories of the 'Old Road', digging into some of the riddles connected with it.

At the time, tackling most of the route unseen, the need to ascend anything remotely steep felt almost adversarial. After, I wanted to understand why there had been so many climbs.

Most straightforwardly, many of the major hills came after a river valley – the Wey, the Mole, the Darent and the Medway.

Sometimes the shape of the escarpment - extreme steepness and deep coombs right down to the foot of the hill - forced the prehistoric and medieval traveller into avoidance action, up to the crest to get around. This was the case with Colley Hill where we were took the historic route (42). And the track up the second steep hill after the A22, originated out of similar obstacle dodging, it helped us circle above the deep railway cutting north of Oxted (43).

We also had to circumnavigate several big estates. The trek up to the top and back down again near Knockholt was a diversion round Chevening Park, the Foreign Secretary's pad (44). Climbing Botley Hill cut out any trespassing across Titsey Place (45). And Winders Hill stopped us traipsing through a vineyard.

In January, I'd helped out on the #SlowWays project – creating new walking routes between British towns (46). This offered up another clue. My little group did North Wales, linking footpaths between Abergele and St Asaph, Llandudno, Colwyn Bay and the like. We were told to avoid narrow country lanes with no room for pedestrians. The North Downs Way developers took a similar safety-first approach. The lane along the bottom of the slope connecting Otford and Wrotham is clearly marked Pilgrim's Way – and using it would have avoided all those nasty steps – but we only dropped onto it once a new road appeared below, taking all the traffic away.

And there was a 'seeking out the scenic route' principle. The section between Detling and Hollingbourne raised eyebrows at the time, but it provided some great views over Holmesdale and offered a contrast to the 14 mile stretch along the foot of the hill which followed.

In that dark hour before dawn, Ade and I felt like we were paying a once-in-a-lifetime penance, emulating those sent on a similar journey as a form of medieval punishment. And a more positive part of the race experience, many of us serendipitously meeting and being helped by strangers, carried one of the obvious hallmarks of a pilgrimage (47). But although our route has been known as the 'Pilgrim's Way' for centuries, there seems to be scant surviving evidence of the original pilgrims using it (48). If anything, the arguments for its use during prehistoric times seem stronger.

The Cathedral records show that between Thomas Becket's demise in 1170 and Henry VIII ordering the destruction of his shrine in 1538, a minimum of several hundred pilgrims a year did visit Canterbury to pay their respects. But logic suggests many chose the direct route described in Chaucer's Canterbury Tales - Watling Street, which runs in a straight line across North Kent (49).

The main advantages of the North Downs option seem to be that it was a navigationally straightforward, long-established route, without the threat of highwaymen that beset the busier Watling Street. But if pilgrims did come our way, they didn't leave much of a trace (50).

The lack of certainty around the provenance of the 'Pilgrims Way' seems to be behind the switch of name for the planned national trail after the Second World War, the reason the powers that be went with the safer 'North Downs Way.' (51) Maybe there's further evidence to uncover, and one day it will become obvious why our route acquired its traditional epithet.

It's an early Sunday morning in late October, almost a year on from Wendover. There's a similar chill in the air - down jacket weather again. An eerie mist is draped in wisps across the crest, giving the autumn colours on the scarp slope a muted feel. A quarter of a mile to the north is the path I took with Zoe and Jane a few months before. Though the memories of that night are strong, I've made my peace with the North Downs now, and I've come to see the Long Barrow at Coldrum. The early Neolithic burial site and Sarsen stones (52). It wasn't easy to find - my maps app got confused and I took a couple of wrong turns up a cul-de-sac of narrow country lanes.

I've lived near, and been connected with the Medway most of my life. Mum and Dad's families both had strong connections with Chatham and Rochester, I spent 15 years near Maidstone growing up, and for the last 20 years I've been working near the river's source in East Sussex. Yet I never knew about the Medway megaliths.

Now I'm here at one of the prehistoric sites for the first time, trying to uncover more about a final riddle, and there's no-one else around. There's a stillness about this place, a powerful kind of quiet - broken from time to time by a blackbird singing. An unseen breeze silently moves the branches of the giant beech tree just below. Stonehenge gets all the attention but Coldrum was constructed a millennium earlier, a mass burial barrow and monument to the ancestors - one of the earliest prehistoric sites surviving in Britain and almost exactly 6,000 years old (53).

The graphs are climbing ominously again and it's easy to blame the pandemic for everything at the moment. But without it I wouldn't have run the North Downs, I wouldn't have ended up here.

Even though the mist is lingering, you can see the line of hills continuing six or seven miles away on the far side of the Medway gap. The cradle of stones at the entrance, and the alignment of the mound, seem shaped to point the way across.

In the race, we did a 15-mile detour up to and over the M2 bridge then back round again, but what about in 4,000 BC? If the contemporaries of the barrow builders used the hills as a landmark for their journeys, how did they navigate across here without them and find a place to ford the river? Look at a map of the megaliths and you can see them clustered on both sides at the bottom of the gap. Clearly this point in the journey was significant, and it seems one of the functions of Coldrum and Kit's Coty – each at exactly the same height above sea level (54) – was to signpost where to go.

Both Hilaire Belloc and Derek Bright weigh up the pros and cons of four possible prehistoric and medieval Medway crossings – Cuxton, Halling, Aylesford and Snodland. The evidence suggests all were possible and in use from time to time, but the indicators for Snodland seem most compelling. It's in a direct line between the megalith sites. A number of Roman artefacts have been found nearby, suggesting the route was a regular thoroughfare by then. And there's a hidden layer of rock just below the surface which allows you to wade across at low tide (55).

Although any remaining evidence now seems lost, there is also a local legend about an avenue of standing stones (56), a set of Neolithic waymarkers from Coldrum to Kit's Coty, guiding people on the Old Road across this their moment of greatest uncertainty...

It's a captivating vision - which part of me wants to believe in. But wouldn't such obvious help have somehow missed the point? When he was exploring the 'Old Ways', Rob Macfarlane found a direct link between the old

English word for 'learn' and an older Germanic word 'liznojan' meaning 'to follow or to find a track.' (57)

To _find_ a track… The North Downs Way was one of the most intense learning experiences of my life. But not because I was shown where to go. In that field before Knockholt, I was far beyond the limits of my previous terms of reference, full of doubt, a hair's breadth away from dropping out of the race. And yet, through a combination of luck, support and kindness from other people, and figuring it out in the heat of the moment, I stumbled on a way forward. Maybe this is one of the reasons why 100 mile races are so addictive, and why we should remember the potential to learn from all forms of adventure, not just ultras.

So, it's a no from me for the standing stones. I prefer to picture our furrowed-brow Neolithic traveller stood in the morning stillness at Coldrum, eyeing the distant ridgeline above the trees and contemplating the uncertainty; then armed with hearsay and living on their wits, setting off to discover their own way across.

ACCOUNTS FROM OTHER RUNNERS

Allie Bailey [25:18:52] 30th place

On race organisation
'This race showed just what humans can do together... It shows how kind and considerate strangers can be to each other even when they are not allowed to touch or be close to each other. It shows how if we really want something to work as a community, with clear instruction and by working together, we can make it work... James was clear, concise and well thought out in his planning. It was a complete masterclass in communication. He explained everything with a calm, serious clarity that gave every runner hope that we could do this. He had covered every what if in the book.'

Coping with the heat early on
'I was drinking a litre of water every 7-8 miles at this point and another 500ml at every checkpoint and taking on salt. It was hideously humid and even though I have done races in very hot climates this was different. The humidity made it feel like I was running in a sauna. Secret weapon was a bag of crisps at every aid station and water not hydro drinks. Keep it simple and plain. Don't upset your stomach. Carry on.'

The crewpoint in Rockshaw Road

'...all the crews were parked up, boots open in the sun, all socially distanced. They were all so kind, cheering on every runner and offering ice and water to every person that went past. They didn't need to do that. This was human nature at its finest. It made my heart sing. People passed ice to me with gloved hands. People offered ice pops and food, their voices muffled by masks. We were doing this. We were making it work... It was love. It was care. It was just incredibly beautiful to be a part of it.'

Accident before Detling

'I was really struggling with tiredness – something I had not encountered on a 100 before – but at times could feel my eyes starting to close. I think it was the heat in the day and the lack of sleep the week before. I just wanted to lay down and sleep for five minutes... I wasn't paying proper attention when Lorna told me to get off the field I was running on and onto the path. The moment she said that, I tripped on a little rock and proper hit the deck, elbow first them left leg and shoulder slamming into the super sold chalk downs... The force of me hitting the ground broke my (now redundant) watch strap. I got up, did the mandatory "is anyone laughing at me" check and dusted myself down. It hurt but I couldn't see any blood, so we kept going. Five minutes later I looked at my leg and blood was dripping onto it from my elbow which was pumping it all down my arm, onto my leg, onto the floor, onto my number. It was everywhere. I got my buff and put some water in it to try and clean it up a bit'

The ups and downs after Detling

'I was so, so tired. It came in waves, waves where I didn't think I could stand up and then suddenly it would disappear. My stomach was threatening me too – again it came in waves. I was getting real ratty. My quads hurt a LOT both from falling over and doing 8,000 ft of elevation hoofing it up Olympus the week before. I had some major doubts about myself and felt like I should have pushed more, but not knowing when the ups and downs would end meant that I held back a bit. And I knew that the sub 24 was now out of the question so my motivation dipped. Lorna was great. Running ahead *and doing her best to keep me going up the massive ups and downs out of Detling. The hallucinations were real too. I saw some well weird shit that definitely wasn't there. I just wanted the dawn to come.'*

The finish
'As the track at Ashford came into sight, I felt an overwhelming sense of relief... I ran the final 400m round the track trying not to cry. The Centurion Army, or a skeleton crew of them, stood masked and clapping at the end. Stuart March in his usual place on the floor. I crossed the line in 25 hours and 18 mins. I placed 30th overall, 5th lady and 2nd in category. Maybe I wasn't as shit as I thought I was. The weather had killed off over half the field bit it hadn't killed me.'

More at www.alliebailey.co.uk/alliebruns/2020/8/12/norths-downs-way-100-a-masterclass-in-organising-and-ultra-in-a-global-pandemic

Dai Davies [27:45:43] 60th place

First rough patch after Colley Hill
'From Reigate was a struggle. I think I've mentally blocked it all out. There was a lot of walking and not too much running. Suffering with early signs of heat exhaustion already, I was slipping into some dark thoughts. I just couldn't get the legs to fire up again. The cramping was persistent. I had a lot of salted food in crisps, salted cashews, pretzels and Tailwind and I hoped at some point it would all kick in. I made it to Merstham and the welcome sight of the wonderful ladies who I volunteered with the year before. They gave me some ice in a little packet which I put under my cap and sent me on my way.'

Boosted by support
'I was dining out on the generous support of familiar faces and strangers alike. That was my energy source... Whilst the soaring summer temperatures took my physical energy, it couldn't beat my

mental strength which was being topped up constantly, something I hadn't planned for. Knockholt saw a massive refill of energy in the familiar shape of Paul Christian. What he was doing all the way out here in Knockholt I did not know. It was great to see him and I'm so grateful for him being there.'

A protector through the night
'I was head down focusing. I wasn't alone in my thoughts though. There was a centurion there too, he was running slightly ahead of me through the woods. He was huge, too big to fit on the path. A bulking mass of metal smashing through the foliage with his gladius. I felt like he was tormenting me, teasing me even. He couldn't speak, he lumbered on aggressively and I could hear the sound of his armour chinking. A sound which drove right through me. Head down and focus I kept thinking. He's not my enemy, only I am. I convinced myself he was here to guide me through the night, I chose to use him, to follow him and accept the thrashing sound of metal in the night. He left me as we emerged from Boxley Wood when a few other speedy runners galloped passed on the downhill as I relied purely on gravity to keep me moving forward.'

The last stretch
'Around the roundabout we walked and then began running again... this was it, this was the end. It was almost in touching distance now… We paced around the track and began smiling as the final straight loomed… I ducked my head as I crossed the finish line… It was over. I'd run a 100 miles for the second time, proving to myself that the first time wasn't a fluke achievement… I finished in 27 hours and 45 minutes, sub 28 hours achieved. I was a centurion now…'

More at https://runwithdai.com/2020/08/16/im-a-centurion-now

Sonny Peart [28:53:31] 90th place

The Centurion community
'Despite the social distancing, I already felt like I was back in the bosom of my running family. Being part of just one Centurion event can be a bonding experience, and last year I ran five and volunteered at four. So this did feel like coming home. I exchanged words with Stuart March and Nici, and Stuart McLaughlin, supervising drop bags, passed on a message from my pacer, Helen Caddy-Leach – "Don't fuck about." Or words to that effect. Similar in tone to the encouraging WhatsApp message from fellow-Black Trail Runners founder, Sabrina Pace-Humphreys – "Don't be shit."'

Tough stretch
'During my 2019 NDW50 run, the seven mile section from Box Hill to Reigate had been the low point of my race. It was much the same this time round. The day had warmed up considerably, the ups and downs were relentless, and my heart rate stayed persistently high even when walking. Trying to cool down, I drank all my fluids. Not filling my extra bottle at Box Hill left me with nothing to drink for more than a mile. Reigate aid station couldn't come soon enough. The passer-by telling me it was 500m ahead was a bloody liar... When the checkpoint finally hove into view, it was lovely to see fellow-Black Trail Runners co-founder Donna Richards on duty.'

Getting the pacing right
'By now it was late afternoon. It was still very hot, and this section of the course has lots of exposed parts, running across and alongside south-facing fields. The race was taking its toll on the runners, and I was starting to gain places, as other runners slowed or dropped out. I moved up 19 places between Box Hill and Botley Hill, and another 12 by the time I reached Knockholt.'

Unexpected support
'Not too far from Knockholt someone shouted my name from up ahead, and I saw that it was my former London Business School

classmate Andrew Cosgrove, and his wife Amanda. The route passed close to their house, and they'd been dot-watching my progress, and came out to give me a cheer. A really nice surprise that put a smile on my face for a good few miles... There was also more general support out on the course. Crews were generous to all runners. A special shout-out to Dimi Booth and her partner, popping up at countless points, distributing Calippos to all and sundry...'

<u>The stretch after Detling</u>
'The four miles after Detling – four miles of shit, as Helen described them as we headed up the first incline out of the village – would be hard work on a cool day, without 82 miles in my legs. On this occasion, they just felt cruel. One could see roads and paths hugging the valley floors, but the NDW always take the 'high road', with endless steps, flinty paths and low hanging branches to stoop under. After about two miles of this morale-sapping slow progress, I was plucking up the courage to suggest we could slow down a bit; I was sure we had sufficient time in the bank, and I was just plain knackered. Helen spoke before I opened my mouth, saying, "Sonny, we need to speed up." I don't think it was by accident that she was out of reach of my poles when she said it.'

<u>Dunn Street to the Finish</u>
'I told Helen I had sub-29 as my new target. The previous day that wouldn't have felt like much to aim at. From here, it felt like an appropriate ambition. It meant running in for the most part, and on paper it would hopefully look like I wasn't chasing cut-offs.

As we entered Ashford, only a broken leg was going to stop me getting a buckle. The last few miles of the race are the antithesis of the previous 100. Suburban roads lead eventually to the Julie Rose Stadium. I didn't know what to expect there, given the adjustments. Would anyone be there? How would it feel to enter the stadium?

The answer was that it felt awesome. Not only the prospect of stopping moving for the first time since Saturday morning, but the now very real, the undeniable prospect of having a NDW100 buckle, and one that few others would have. I was sorely tempted to walk round the track, but Helen would not hear of it, so we jogged round those last few hundred metres. There were quite a few people sitting around the perimeter of the track.... I could hear applause, and I felt like I'd earned it. I raised my arms, poles in one hand, as I crossed the finish line under the familiar blue Centurion arch. One yard further on, I fell to the floor in relief and exhaustion'

More here www.son966.wixsite.com/unknownbeauty/single-post/a-long-distance-social-event

Dave Stuart [25:15:04] 28th place

The Devil's Cornfield
'A couple of miles later, it was the "Dave steps" – normally I would be giving out drinks and Percy pigs but I was too busy running today. I also knew this would be the hottest section of the entire race. It is a South facing escarpment so there would be no hiding from the sun. The clouds had cleared and it was strong sunshine. To make matters worse, it is a chalk field section which reflects the sun so you get cooked from both sides.... Strava booked this as being 97f / 36c. This was a genuine temperature reading...'

Between Otford and Wrotham
'I remembered from last time that there is an awful hill out of Otford. The trail turns off basically into someone's drive and straight up a wall. I had remembered it from 2016 and wasn't impressed that year. The climb to Otford mount is ridiculous. However there was a surprise this year. A little girl was spraying the runners with a hosepipe. Normally a hosepipe to the face at point blank range would be awful but this was majestic and kept me cool for quite a while...

I traded places with a few people including Giacomo – next time we will have to get some on course gelato...

I overtook a lady and her daughter pacer. She seemed to be struggling and overtook her quite easily. She had a second wind and overtook me a mile or so later. I used them to pull myself along toward Wrotham...

I also overtook some monks on their way to Canterbury. You do see some strange sights on the trails...'

Climbing Bluebell Hill
'The temperature picked up quite a bit coming up the side of Bluebell Hill despite being well after dark. This was a bit of a low point. I often find I hit lows around the crew points — I was running low on supplies and still had a mile or two to go. Having a crew must be nice to have a few extra snacks and cool drink refills. I think today it could potentially have been a big benefit with the limited range of food at the CPs and COVID protocols... I had an unusual mental boost here — I caught sight of a badger in the field and it ran straight across in front of me. It was quite a small one and ran away. It made me a smile and helped on towards the CP'

Trying to beat Ken Fancett
'Ken and I have done 10 Centurion races together and Ken had beaten me every time by between 1 and 3 hours. Ken is a living legend and despite being over 70 is one of the best runners even in absolute terms in the Centurion series…

It is smooth road and pavement for the last 3 miles with a gentle downhill trend. I was pushing as hard as could — I had the thought of finishing ahead of Ken and seeing how much I could beat last time. I was pushing hard and running hard whenever I could see tape.

Miles 101 and 102 were 10:27 and 10:30…

I was pushing hard round the track as it looked like I could sneak under the very arbitrary 25:15 mark but just missed it at 25:15:04. I was 25th finisher over the line and had the "club house" lead over Ken.

As I was getting ready to leave, Ken was came trotting round the track. Unless he had started just before 7am, I had beaten him. As he crossed the line, I waited for the results to refresh. I had beaten him by just over 6 minutes. Ken 10, Dave 1!'

More here www.76thmile.blogspot.com/2020/08/2020-centurion-north-downs-way-100

Ashley Varley [19:51:43] 2nd place

'My time at the 2020 North Downs Way 100 would have given me a finishing position of between approximately 10th and 20th place at the last three NDW100 races. But... somehow, this year, it was good enough for second overall!! I am no elite ultrarunner and I have never placed anywhere near that high before – and I doubt I will again. But luck was on my side in 2020 and I will forever be able to say that once – just once – I finished in second place at a 100 mile race! When I look at the results, I still can't believe that my name is there, just behind the winner!

For me, these races are very much a team thing, and to that end, I have to thank a few people. Firstly, my beautiful wife, Jane, who was my crew for the day. Jane kept me fed and watered and gave me endless encouraging hugs! I love you, honey. My incredible pacer, Paul McCleery who joined me at Bluebell Hill. He got me through the Detling Hills and when I was flagging around Charing, he kept me moving until I found the inner strength to push on to the end. Paul is so much more than a pacer, he is an inspiration and a great friend. And of course, the amazing Centurion volunteers. As ever, you were all friendly, encouraging, kind, thoughtful and full of cheers and smiles. You were the Guinea Pigs for a new way of doing things this year, and you did it like you had been doing it for years. Thank you all so much.

I have been running for about 15 years now and I've reached the ripe old age of 48! During the last three years I have worked hard on improving and maximising my training. The result has been new personal bests from 5k up to marathon distance and I have discovered the brilliance of ultra-running. And with a bit of luck, I managed a result at the NDW100 that was beyond my wildest dreams! The only advice I can offer is, work hard, believe in yourself and never stop dreaming. You never know what you might achieve! I mean – this dog has had its day!'

Paul Schnell [27:52:17] 63rd place

Bad patch just after half-way

'The next stretch to the Otford crew point was my worst. I wasn't in bad physical shape but I started get get a flood of negative thoughts. "This is too big", "you're only half way", " you have the whole night ahead", "you don't have to finish, no one cares one way or the other"... A bunch of nosy rubbish like that. It just kept playing on repeat and started to erode my mood. I started finding reasons to drop.

About a mile or two out of the aid station I had a tachycardia heart episode. I've lived with this condition my whole life which causes my heart-rate to rocket up to around 220 bpm for a spell. It's an electrical irregularity (rather than a physiological problem) and I can usually bring it under control with controlled breathing. I don't generally get it while running but it has happened on occasion and is a bit unsettling. This time I was struggling to control it. More fuel for the drop out fire. It did eventually correct and I continued on wrapped up in a cloud of doubt.'

Feeling better after Otford

'This is where things got strange. This is the part I don't understand. Leaving Otford you head immediately up a really nasty climb. In parts with steps. I thought "sheesh! really! give me a damn break". But, I kept moving. My legs were working, I just kept powering up. Something flipped in my head up that hill. I went from negative to positive... I got to the top and found myself in farmland with the sun going down. It was just beautiful...

From here to the aid station at Wrotham I just kept pushing, much of it running comfortably. Everything had turned around. Cally will tell you – she was really worried at Otford but saw a different person arrive at Wrotham. I knew I could do this. The belief in the finish was there. There was less uncertainty. 40 miles to go! I can do this'

The finish
'What a joy to hit the track at the stadium. It's such an awesome way to finish the race. The only thing missing was probably Chariots of fire blaring out of the PA – no trouble, I had cued up Pink Floyd "Comfortably numb" in my headphones. It was a perfect finish...

I'm so grateful to have been able to run and finish this event. It was such a huge challenge. I'm amazed at how my body responded to the task. Just a few weeks prior I had called it off feeling that I was not ready – just shows that we capable of so much more. It's a trite thing to say but when you experience it first-hand the meaning becomes apparent.'

More here www.12in12in2020.com/2020/08/12/8-north-downs-way-100-mile

Ally Whitlock [26:45:09] 48th place

Early on
'In the cool of the early morning the first ten miles speed by. It's effortless running. The trails are wide, well-marked & easy underfoot. The legs fresh & keen to get going. I may not have run this part of the trail since the NDW50 in 2018 but my feet seem to instinctively remember the way.'

Between Newland and Westhumble
'As the miles tick by I find I don't have to think about what I am doing too much, which I like. The trail is familiar enough that I only have to glance at the markings every now & again to know I'm on route. The underfoot conditions are good... Nothing against anyone else, but at this moment in time I am liking the serenity of my own company & my own thoughts...'

On the volunteers
'I ask Lou how she's finding it & she says it's tough. Her natural reaction is to help & she can't. She's also a hugger & isn't able to touch the runners.

This sentiment was repeated time & time again by volunteers at *all the check-points. They wanted to do MORE for us, not less. It pained them to see runners struggling & to not be able to help, whether than be filling a tired runner's bottles or helping a limping runner deal with blisters.*

But this is simply the Centurion Army way. The races would not happen without the volunteers, Many of whom, especially at the latter check-points, are giving up whole days & nights of their time to support us runners. And what a job they did under difficult conditions. Every CP was superbly organised, fully stocked & every volunteer cheery, supportive & encouraging – even those wearing PPE in 30+ degree temperatures for hours on end. They deserve a buckle for that to be honest.'

Between miles 40 and 50

'Everyone I pass, and everyone who passes me is slightly dazed, almost confused, struggling in the heat. Hardly anyone is running more than a few steps at a time. I keep crossing paths with the same people as we have surges of energy & lulls at different times. Rounding one field, I look behind me to a line of despondent, tired runners, simply trying to put one foot in front of the other.'

Bluebell Hill

'Up, and up, and up. I don't remember this hill dragging on this much. I am exhausted. My eyes are struggling to stay open. So, so tired. I need to sit down. I see a concrete block on the side of the path. I lean on it. Stubbornness scolds me for being so weak. On I move. Up, and up, and up. Slower, and slower, and slower. I'm feeling very nauseous. And tired. So tired.

I sit down where I am. Right in the middle of the path. I'm not sure Helen knows what to do. I'm convinced I'm done. I want to lie down & sleep. My stomach churns. The familiar feeling. I jump up, I need a bush… There are no bushes, just brambles. I fight my way through a few, scratching my legs as I try to be at least a little discrete. For the second time, I leave my guts on the NDW.

Just like outside Knockholt the nausea instantly lifts. My doubts clear & I'm ready to go. I fight my way back out of the brambles, pick up my poles & carry on up the hill towards the next CP.'

Nailing it

'To hear that I am doing quite well is the push I need. There's a sparkle in my eye, a spring in my step & a smile on my face. I am doing this! I subconsciously pick up the pace as I feel the draw of the finish line. Spencer looks at his watch & tells me that 90 odd miles into the race we are clocking 10-minute mile pace.

I feel great. No, scrap that, I feel AMAZING! I keep on running. Running, running, running… I feel good enough to run some of the smaller hills. Gentle inclines that I was walking up in the first ten miles I'm running up in the last ten…

We're running through Ashford now. Along quiet residential roads. Past a pub. A school. Maybe a mile to go. I feel a lump in my throat & I begin to choke up. I fear for a moment that I am going to start crying again. At mile 97 of the SDW, it was pain & frustration that saw me cry. Any tears here would be tears of happiness as I realise the enormity of what I have done…

My stomach turns in nervous anticipation as I see the sign 'this way to the finish'. Turning into the stadium grounds I hear the excited buzz of the finish area. I hold myself back for a moment & take a deep breath. A few quiet words as I compose myself.

I've done it.

Through the gates & onto the track. Helen waving & cheering me on. As my feet hit the cushioned surface I don't even think as I instinctively start to run faster. Along the back straight I move into lane one. Rounding the final corner, the finish gantry a mere 100 meters away. I break into a sprint as my smile widens. I'm trying to take it all in, to savour the moment. After 103+ miles, I am not simply running, but I am sprinting for that finish.

I cross the line, eyes closed in complete & utter exhilaration.

I had three goals for the North Downs Way; to enjoy it, to finish strong & run with a smile. I gave that race my everything. I cross the line knowing that I have just run the race of my life.

At this moment in time, there is no better feeling.'

More here www.photogirlruns.blog/2020/08/20/ndw100

THANK YOU

I want to acknowledge and say a huge and heartfelt thank you to the people who helped me during the race and in the writing of this book. In particular to...

...Dan Park & Lesley Lewis at Knockholt – you made my year!

...The other volunteer who helped talk me round at Knockholt. I'm sorry I don't yet know your name, but you made a difference too!

...The 'ice lady' at Wrotham – I will remember your 'random' act of kindness for the rest of my life

...All of the 95 volunteers and Centurion staff who created this triumph of humanity, putting on a safe and supportive event under extremely challenging and unprecedented circumstances during the weekend of 7th-8th August 2020 including James Elson, Nicci Griffin, Stuart Mills, Anna Troop, Sinead Bradbeer, Lou Fraser, Graham Carter, Stu McLoughlin

...Liz for coming to get me from Ashford and coming to meet me in Ashford, being a legend through the rough patch, providing enjoyable company on Wednesday night runs and helping develop the 'pause in the Anthropocene' idea in this book

...Ian, Louise and Heather for totally having my back through the Fantastic Four thread. Ian for your calmness and care during the phonecall, Louise for your coaching session, and Heather for the

beautiful debrief walk round Balcombe

...Michael and Michelle for coming out to see if I was alright and the care you showed at the time

...Spencer for geeing my up in Wrotham at a crucial moment and helping me take things less seriously and for helping Ally during her run of a lifetime (and Helen too!)

...Zoe and Jane, Keri, Ade, Giacomo, Darren, Sam, and Rob for your company during the race

...Rob for always being inspirational

...Dai, Sonny, Dave, Ashley, Allie, Paul and Ally for giving me permission to include and edit your race reports

...Ivor for calmly pointing me in the right direction on the recce, and for all the advice in your NDW100 blogs

...Pete and Emma and everyone at Hindleap for your messages of support when you had more important things to worry about

...Steve Dewar for listening to me talking about the book, encouraging my writing and helping develop the ideas around adventure

...Danny Shoultz for your support and friendship and making sure I stay on the right track

...Clare Downey for online scrabble during lockdown

...Paul 'Ace' Brookshaw for your company on the first North Downs Way recce in Summer 2019

...Jim and Tine at Lowthwaite B&B for helping me recover from the shin injury in double quick time and for your empathy and hospitality

...The lady on Seat Sandal for your wisdom at just the right time

...Laura for your free physiotherapy advice and ongoing interest in ultrarunning and caring support for my efforts

...Louise again, and Andrew Cooper and Jon Gray and Sally Marsh for offering to read the book. And Andrew thank you for your advice about the writing mirroring the rhythm of the run

...Brian Drought for showing us around the Wendover loop and for your support during the race

...Anna Troop, Stu McLoughlin, Kerry Cooper, Ian Hammett and all those who volunteered on Wendover Woods 50 2019

...and finally, Ilaria, thank you for being my soulmate

REFERENCES

1. From Theodore Roosevelt's 'Man in a Republic' speech made at the Sorbonne in Paris on 23rd April 2010. Sourced via www.worldfuturefund.org/Documents/maninarena
2. The benefits of this are explained in 'One Day by the Thames' (Uckfield: Amazon KDP, 2019)
3. There's an excellent example of how to do a DNF postmortem properly in John Morelock, 'Run Gently Out There' (Whidbey Island: Amazon KDP, 2013) pp.41-46
4. You'll find these if you search 'North Downs Way 100' on www.youtube.com. I watched the films made by Ben Parkes, Daz Staley and Adam Lucas-Lucas.
5. www.centurionrunning.com/blog/2019/10/23/wendover-woods-50-2020-notes-for-runners
6. www.centurionrunning.com/reports/2019/2019-ww50-race-report
7. See John Curtin & Henry Stedman, 'North Downs Way' (Hindhead: Trailblazer Publications, 2018) p.11 and Derek Bright, 'The Pilgrims' Way – Fact and Fiction of an Ancient Trackway' (Stroud: The History Press, 2011) pp.79-89
8. https://www.youtube.com/watch?v=x3k9t9i-TU4 or search '2020 North Downs Way 100 Race Briefing' on www.youtube.com

9. https://vimeo.com/180644342 or search 'Rob's 100 mile record attempt'. This is one of the most uplifting videos I've ever seen please watch it!

10. Hilaire Belloc, 'The Old Road' (Createspace Independent Publishing, 2014 - first published 1904)

11. John Curtin & Henry Stedman, 'North Downs Way' (Hindhead: Trailblazer Publications, 2018)

12. www.surreyhills.org/surrey-hills-60/st-marthas-church

13. John Curtin & Henry Stedman, 'North Downs Way' (Hindhead: Trailblazer Publications, 2018) p.88

14. Attunement to nature, and 'the loss of the sense of barriers between oneself and nature...' is one of the 'rewards' of being along covered in Sara Maitland, 'How to Be Alone' (London: Macmillan, 2014) p.123

15. This beautiful book was part of our reading list – Magnus Magnusson, 'Rum: Nature's Island' (Edinburgh: Luath Press Ltd, 1997)

16. Adharanand Finn, 'The Way of the Runner' (London: Faber & Faber, 2015) p.305

17. www.centurionrunning.com/reports/2020/2020-one-community-event-report

18. www.randomforestrunner.com/2020/07/a-new-pennine-way-record – worth reading in full. Here is a flavour 'I truly believe that we are all capable of so much more than we believe we are. In most things, we are so far from the edge of our true limits that we're not even within sight of where they are.'

19. https://www.youtube.com/watch?v=sUgpAL87E5Q or search 'Breaking The Pennine Way Record - Damian Hall' in Google videos

20. There's a lot superficial material online about Sabrina's Pennine Way FKT and Wainwright round accomplishments but I would recommend her interview on the British Ultra Running Podcast Episode 31 for a proper insight into her mindset

21. At the time of going to press Dave MacFarlane's film about Dan's JOGLE record was due out any day. If this teaser is anything to go by https://vimeo.com/449432349 it will be a cracker. Keep an eye on dmtwo.media for the full film

22. https://ultrarunningcommunity.com/13-report/445-328-ndw100-north-downs-way-100-race-report or search 'Traviss Willcox North Downs Race Report' online

23. Deena Kastor, 'Let Your Mind Run' (New York: Three Rivers Press, 2018)

24. 'One Day by the Thames' (Uckfield: Amazon KDP, 2019) p.68

25. https://gcgoesultra.wordpress.com/2019/08/11/north-downs-way-100-redemption-time/

26. www.hindleapwarren.org

27. See note 9

28. See note 1

29. Hilaire Belloc, 'The Old Road' (Createspace Independent Publishing, 2014 - first published 1904) p.79

30. www.otfordpalace.org/announcement/the-king-visits/

31. www.photogirlruns.blog/2020/08/20/ndw100

32. Derek Bright points out that most modern travellers follow the historic direction of travel along here in 'The Pilgrims' Way – Fact and Fiction of an Ancient Trackway' (Stroud: The History Press, 2011) p.24

33. www.mudcrew.co.uk/event/the-arc-of-attrition/

34. North Downs Way National Trail, Harvey Maps

35. Derek Bright, 'The Pilgrims' Way – Fact and Fiction of an Ancient Trackway' (Stroud: The History Press, 2011) p.89

36. www.lowthwaiteullswater.com

37. Derek Bright, 'The Pilgrims' Way – Fact and Fiction of an Ancient Trackway' (Stroud: The History Press, 2011) p.90 for the details about the phials and Beckitt's 'blood'

38. As per note 36 pp.86-87 for the story of Henry II's trip to Canterbury

39. Robert Macfarlane, 'The Old Ways' (London: Penguin, 2012) p. 40 'The first foot-travellers to enter Britain almost certainly crossed over on chalk, which provided the land bridge with what is now Europe'

40. As per note 38, p.40

41. James Elson's Race Director write up is here https://www.centurionrunning.com/reports/2020/ndw100-2020-

race-report. James also talked through what happened on the Run to the Hills video about the race on Youtube https://www.youtube.com/watch?v=NwY_GD_6Rns

42. As per note 10, pp.70-71

43. As per note 10, pp.77-78

44. As per note 10, p.79

45. As per note 10, p.78

46. www.slowways.uk

47. www.theguardian.com/lifeandstyle/2020/oct/31/in-troubled-times-a-ritual-walk-can-clear-the-mind-and-soothe-the-soul

48. This is basically the main argument of Derek Bright's book – reference details note 34

49. As per note 34. Derek Bright's book ends with some very impressive and detailed calculations about how many pilgims visited Thomas Beckitt's shrine

50. As per note 34

51. As per note 34 see p.73

52. www.nationaltrust.org.uk/coldrum-long-barrow

53. This info gathered from the National Trust information boards onsite at Coldrum

54. As per note 34, p.111

55. Covered in detail in both the Belloc and Bright books – reference details notes 10 and 34

56. As per note 34, p.111

57. As per note 38, p.31

Printed in Great Britain
by Amazon